THE SEQUEL

How to Change Your Career Without Starting Over

Laurence Shatkin, Ph.D.

THE SEQUEL: HOW TO CHANGE YOUR CAREER WITHOUT STARTING OVER

© 2011 by JIST Publishing

Published by JIST Works, an imprint of JIST Publishing
7321 Shadeland Station, Suite 200
Indianapolis, IN 46256-3923

Phone: 800-648-JIST   Fax: 877-454-7839
E-mail: info@jist.com   Website: www.jist.com

Some Other Books by Laurence Shatkin, Ph.D.

Best Jobs for the 21st Century	40 Best Fields for Your Career
200 Best Jobs for College Graduates	225 Best Jobs for Baby Boomers
300 Best Jobs Without a Four-Year Degree	250 Best-Paying Jobs
200 Best Jobs Through Apprenticeships	150 Best Jobs for a Better World
50 Best Jobs for Your Personality	200 Best Jobs for Introverts

Quantity discounts are available for JIST products. Please call 800-648-JIST or visit www.jist.com for a free catalog and more information.

Visit www.jist.com for information on JIST, tables of contents, sample pages, and ordering information on our many products.

Acquisitions Editor: Susan Pines
Development Editor: Stephanie Koutek
Cover Designer: Honeymoon Image & Design, Inc.
Interior Layout: Toi Davis
Proofreaders: Chuck Hutchinson, Jeanne Clark
Indexer: Cheryl Lenser

Printed in the United States of America

16 15 14 13 12 11   9 8 7 6 5 4 3 2 1

Library of Congress Cataloging-in-Publication Data

Shatkin, Laurence.
    The sequel : how to change your career without starting over / Laurence Shatkin.
        p. cm.
    Includes index.
    ISBN 978-1-59357-865-7 (alk. paper)
    1. Career changes. 2. Career development. I. Title.
    HF5384.S53 2011
    650.14--dc22
                                                2010054488

We have been careful to provide accurate information throughout this book, but it is possible that errors and omissions have been introduced. Please consider this in making any career plans or other important decisions. Trust your own judgment above all else and in all things.

ISBN 978-1-59357-865-7

Make Your Next Job the Sequel to Your Previous Job

Through work experience, you've learned a lot about your field. You "speak the language," understand what makes the difference between good work and hack work, and know who the major players are. You recognize what buyers want and you know a lot of people. Why jettison all this hard-won knowledge when you plan your next career move?

Instead, make your next job the *sequel* to your previous job. Do something different that uses the knowledge and skills you already have.

This book will open your eyes to a wide range of sequel careers—in management, communications, education, sales, standards enforcement, and several other job functions. You'll find an overview of each sequel career and detailed descriptions of 100 related occupations. You'll also get pointers for how to research a sequel career, get relevant work experience, and find a job in it.

Credits and Acknowledgments: While the author created this book, it is based on the work of many others. The occupational information is based on data obtained from the U.S. Department of Labor and the Census Bureau. These sources provide the most authoritative occupational information available.

Contents

Chapter 3: The Teaching Sequel 39

Chapter 4: The Advocacy Sequel 73

Chapter 5: The Standards-Enforcement Sequel 87

Chapter 6: The Communications Sequel 111

Chapter 7: The Sales Sequel 123

Your Career—The Sequel

Thinking of changing your career? Maybe you're not happy with what you're doing now. Maybe you recently lost your job—or expect to lose it soon. Whatever the reason is, your question now is this: "What's next?"

I want you to think about your future as **the sequel** to what you've been doing so far. Call it "Your Career II" (or III or even IV). But maybe you don't understand what I mean by a **sequel career**. Let me explain.

What a Sequel Career Is

Hollywood loves sequels. There have been nine *Nightmare on Elm Street* movies, seven *Star Wars* releases, six *Rocky* slugfests, six *Saw* horrorfests, and a new *Batman* film about every three years.

Have you ever wondered why sequels are so popular? It's because the movie-going public *knows what to expect*. Think about how you react to the announcement of another *Star Trek* movie. You're already familiar with the characters, the setting for the story, and the type of action that takes place. If you like any of these aspects of the series, you're already interested in seeing the next sequel. The Hollywood studio's publicity campaign is much, much easier than it would be for a completely new concept.

Now think about what kind of *job* you might try for next. Take a hint from the movie studios and find a job where you know what to expect, the kind of job I call a *sequel career*. This is **a career that has a different use for the knowledge and skills you've acquired in your old job**. Like a Hollywood sequel, it carries over much that is familiar from your first effort.

What You Can Learn from This Book

The purpose of this book is to get you to think about and plan for a sequel career. The book introduces you to seven common career groups where you can stage your sequel, plus five more that are described more briefly. It presents detailed facts about 100 representative occupations that can be entered as sequels. It also gives specific suggestions for how to explore possible sequel careers and eventually find a job in one of them.

First, you need to appreciate why a sequel career may be right for you. Turn to the first chapter and find out.

CHAPTER 1

Why It's Smart to Use Your Existing Knowledge and Skills in a Sequel Career

As you saw in the introduction, a sequel career is one that uses the knowledge and skills you acquired in your previous job. You may not be fully aware of how valuable this background can be in your next career.

Advantages You Bring to a Sequel Career

Here are some of the specific advantages you bring to a sequel career. They're phrased in terms of knowledge, but you may also regard some of them as skills:

- You know the terminology of your industry and can "speak the language" of people in that field.

- You know common problems that workers deal with, along with shortcuts and resources that help get the job done.

- You know the standards of quality in the industry and can tell the difference between good and bad output.

- You know the features that purchasers look for in the products and services of the industry.

- You know who and where the major buyers and sellers are: where the industry gets its inputs and where it markets its outputs.

- You know the typical range of prices in the industry.

- You know which organizations dominate the industry and who the up-and-coming outfits are.

- You know how and why the industry is changing, both in its yearly cycle and in its long-term trends.

- You know the regulatory and infrastructure environments of the industry.

- You know what kinds of workers the industry employs and what backgrounds they tend to come from.

- You know the channels of communication that the industry uses.

- You know a lot of people in the industry.

That's a lot of useful knowledge! Any one of these types of knowledge could serve as the foundation for a new job—a job that's different from your old job but that carries over a lot of this knowledge that is familiar to you. In other words, it could be the basis of a *sequel career.*

Still not convinced? Then ask yourself this: Am I really willing to jettison all that hard-won knowledge? Think of how much this knowledge will help you when you hunt for a job opening in a sequel career:

- You'll have an excellent network of people in the industry to feed you information about job openings, including those that are not yet advertised.

- You'll know which employers are the best to work for and the most likely to be hiring.

- You'll know what language to use in your resume and cover letter that will be most impressive to employers in the industry.

These same advantages will carry over to job interviews.

Right now, you may be thinking, "Wait a minute! I'm very familiar with my old job and everything that it involves. But I want to (or have to) do *something else.*"

That's okay, because a sequel career *is* something else. Even though it uses knowledge from your old job, it's a different kind of job. Often it involves somewhat different skills from what you have been doing. For example, if you have been working in a technical field and now want to pursue a career as a technical writer, you're going to need writing skills. Not everybody has those skills or can learn them easily. And not everybody is interested in writing for a living.

How This Book Can Help You Choose a Sequel Career

That's why you'll want to look at the information in Chapters 2 through 9. Each chapter covers a particular kind of sequel career and shows you the important characteristics of that sequel: the major work tasks involved and the environment in which the work gets done. You'll also see the pros and cons of the sequel career and how you might prepare for it.

Each chapter includes descriptions of specific occupations in which you can pursue the kind of sequel described in the chapter. (The appendix identifies the sources of the information.) View these job descriptions as samples and not as a definitive list of possible sequel careers. For some sequels (such as management), there wasn't enough room to include all the examples that are available from the Department of Labor's databases of career information. For other sequels, these databases provide only a handful of examples, but you may be able to think of others, based on your knowledge of your industry.

Of course, a sequel career is not advisable for everyone. Hollywood is not interested in making a sequel to *Son of the Sheik* or *Destry Rides Again*. These are stories that were once very popular but no longer capture the imagination of moviegoers.

Similarly, if your industry is going extinct, you may want to move away from it. But very few industries die out altogether. For example, manufacturing in the United States has shed thousands of low-skilled jobs in recent years, but the industry continues to support many highly skilled jobs and is creating new ones. It's leaner and meaner. Most existing industries will continue to provide jobs in many work roles, especially those that require a high level of skill. Some of these work roles will represent a change from what you're doing now—in other words, a sequel career.

Which Sequel Is Right for You?

Chapters 2 through 8 discuss seven different sequels in detail. (Chapter 9 takes a quick look at five more.) I hope you'll want to browse through every chapter, but you may need a quicker way to decide which sequel might be a good choice for you.

A good way to narrow down your choices is to look at the **skills** that the sequel careers require. Actually, they all require a high level of skill with speaking, writing, critical thinking, and reading comprehension. Most of the jobs in these sequel careers are well above the entry level, so it's not surprising that all require you to be good at acquiring information, making sense of it, and communicating it.

So let's look just at the skills that **differentiate** the various sequel careers—the skills that each sequel requires at a higher level than the average for all sequel careers. These skills characterize the sequels best.

For each sequel, the following table lists the most prominent skills and the chapter where you can read about the sequel. Look at the skills listed here and decide which sequels are the best match for your abilities. If you're not sure what the title of the skill means, find its definition in the last section of the appendix.

Sequel	Differentiating Skills	Chapter
Advocacy	Writing; Speaking; Persuasion; Active Listening; Critical Thinking; Speaking	4
Brokerage	Mathematics; Persuasion; Active Listening; Judgment and Decision Making; Speaking; Negotiation	8
Communications	Writing; Reading Comprehension; Active Listening; Speaking; Critical Thinking; Active Learning	6
Management	Management of Financial Resources; Management of Material Resources; Quality Control Analysis; Management of Personnel Resources; Troubleshooting; Operation Monitoring	2
Sales	Negotiation; Persuasion; Service Orientation; Active Listening; Operation and Control; Installation	7
Standards Enforcement	Science; Troubleshooting; Quality Control Analysis; Operation Monitoring; Systems Analysis; Operations Analysis	5

| Teaching | Learning Strategies; Science; Instructing; Writing; Reading Comprehension; Monitoring | 3 |

Now, turn to the appropriate chapters for the sequel careers that seem right for you. See what the sequels involve and what specific occupations you might consider entering. Also, be sure to look at Chapter 9 for some additional ideas about sequels you might possibly pursue.

CHAPTER 2

The Management Sequel

Management is probably the most common sequel career of them all. Every industry has managers, and competent workers are often encouraged to make a career move to management. This sequel is so obvious that you may wonder why it's even included in this book. The main reason is to get you to weigh both the pros *and cons* of this career route.

What Managers Do

Every organization has a limited supply of resources, including money, physical assets, workers, and time. Some other resources that you might not have thought much about are the goodwill of the public, the ability to conduct operations within the laws, the security of the company, and information about both the company and the outside world. In a large organization, specialized managers ride herd on each of these concerns. These managers create budgets, arrange for loans, decide on investments, set sales targets, develop work schedules, acquire a workforce with the necessary skills, monitor the condition of equipment, develop purchasing schedules, write the corporate mission statement, ensure that the company gets good publicity, keep track of regulations affecting the company, develop security procedures, and organize information that the company uses.

The O*NET database (developed for the U.S. Department of Labor) includes 82 civilian occupations with the word "Manager" or "Management" in the title. In the table at the end of Chapter 1, you saw the most prominent skills that O*NET lists for the managerial occupations. Now, also from O*NET, here are the most important **work activities** that you would do as a manager:

- Developing specific goals and plans to prioritize, organize, and accomplish your work.

- Developing constructive and cooperative working relationships with others; maintaining them over time.

- Handling complaints, settling disputes, and resolving grievances and conflicts or otherwise negotiating with others.

- Providing information to supervisors, co-workers, and subordinates by telephone, in written form, through e-mail, or in person.

- Getting members of a group to work together to accomplish tasks.

- Analyzing information and evaluating results to choose the best solution and solve problems.

- Providing guidance and direction to subordinates, including setting performance standards and monitoring performance.

- Identifying the developmental needs of others and coaching, mentoring, or otherwise helping others to improve their knowledge or skills.

- Scheduling events, programs, and activities, as well as the work of others.

- Keeping up to date technically and applying new knowledge to your job.

The Pros and Cons of Management

For most workers, the main advantage of going into management is that your earnings go up, often considerably. The Bureau of Labor Statistics provides earnings surveys and outlook projections for 46 occupations with the word "Manager" or "Management" in the title. Workers in these occupations earn an average of $74,154, compared to an average of $36,963 for all other occupations. In addition, managerial rank often qualifies you for extra rewards, such as a private office (instead of a cubicle) or a reserved spot in the parking lot.

The BLS projects 7.8% growth for the management occupations from 2008 to 2018 and an average of 9,863 job openings per year. This is slower-than-average growth, and the job openings are far fewer than in many of the occupations that managers supervise—no surprise, because only a small number of workers can climb the career pyramid to the managerial level.

The O*NET database reports these **work environment** characteristics for the managerial occupations:

- Freedom to Make Decisions

- Structured versus Unstructured Work

- Frequency of Decision Making

- Indoors, Environmentally Controlled

- Impact of Decisions on Co-workers or Company Results

- Responsibility for Outcomes and Results

- Time Pressure

- Importance of Being Exact or Accurate

- Responsible for Others' Health and Safety

- Frequency of Conflict Situations

From this list, you can see both the pluses and minuses that managers live with: They get more opportunities to make independent decisions, but they must accept responsibility for the consequences of those decisions. That can be stressful when things go wrong. Another source of stress is the sensitive interpersonal situations they sometimes have to deal with. They may have to fire a worker, get two workers to stop feuding, or tell a worker to bathe more frequently. Managers also tend to work longer hours, which can put a strain on family life. Even when they're not at work, managers may be thinking about work-related issues. Managerial work offers the satisfaction of getting a lot of different elements—people, data, and things—to work together and produce a result. Managers are usually respected by the public, if not by every worker who reports to them.

How to Move into Management

In 1969, Dr. Laurence J. Peter and Raymond Hull wrote an amusing but fundamentally serious book about management, *The Peter Principle,* in which they explained why businesses so often have incompetent managers. They said that competent workers are promoted until they reach a level of responsibility that is more than they can handle. Then they remain there, at their "level of incompetence," muddling through their jobs just well enough to keep from being fired.

There's a lot of truth to that theory. Some people go into management even though they lack the necessary skills to do the job well. The higher pay and status are tempting, and they may even get encouragement to make the switch because they are highly competent at their present non-managerial job. But the promotion to management is often very different from being promoted one step higher as a technician, salesworker, or clerk. It requires a special set of skills that many people are incapable of handling or simply don't enjoy using.

That's why you might want to take a toe-in-the-water approach if you're considering a sequel career in management. Ask your boss to let you take on one managerial responsibility while you're still in your present job. If you handle that task competently and find the work satisfying, try another managerial task. For specific suggestions for opening this discussion with your manager, see Chapter 11.

If you're presently out of work or your manager won't let you take on a managerial task, you may be able to try out a managerial role as a volunteer in a political, social, sports, religious, or neighborhood organization. Find out what the organization does that uses budgeting, scheduling, communications, personnel management, negotiating, or analytical skills. Then offer to serve on the appropriate committee. For example, to use budgeting skills, volunteer for the finance committee. In Chapter 11, you'll find a script you can follow to volunteer your services.

An appropriate bachelor's or master's degree can also open the door to management. In a program of this kind, you can learn skills that might be difficult to acquire from on-the-job or volunteer experience—for example, quantitative methods for making decisions or principles of business law. You may be able to find a program that focuses on your particular industry, such as engineering management, public relations management, or printing management.

It should be obvious now what skills you have to emphasize on your resume when you apply for a managerial job. Your technical knowledge of your industry is still important, but you have to be able to show that you are skilled with specific managerial functions. Remember that you don't get promoted or hired on the basis of what you *might* be able to do, but rather on the basis of skills you have already demonstrated. Numbers are very effective on a resume, so you should brandish numbers that indicate your accomplishments using managerial skills. For example, you could mention the dollar size of the budget you planned or the number of people whose work you scheduled. The best evidence of all is a dollar amount that your efforts earned or saved for the business or volunteer organization.

Descriptions of Managerial Occupations

This book does not have enough room to include descriptions of all 82 managerial occupations in the O*NET database, but here are profiles of 27 jobs that represent a wide variety of fields.

Administrative Services Managers

- Annual Earnings: $75,520
- Earnings Growth Potential: High
- Job Growth: 12.5%
- Annual Job Openings: 8,660
- Self-Employed: 0.2%

Plan, direct, or coordinate supportive services of an organization, such as recordkeeping, mail distribution, telephone operator/receptionist, and other office support services. May oversee facilities planning and maintenance and custodial operations. Direct or coordinate the supportive services department of a business, agency, or organization. Prepare and review operational reports and schedules to ensure accuracy and efficiency. Set goals and deadlines for the department. Acquire, distribute, and store supplies. Analyze internal processes and recommend and implement procedural or policy changes to improve operations, such as supply changes or the disposal of records. Plan, administer, and control budgets for contracts, equipment, and supplies. Monitor the facility to ensure that it remains safe, secure, and well maintained. Hire and terminate clerical and administrative personnel. Oversee the maintenance and repair of machinery, equipment, and electrical and mechanical systems. Oversee construction and renovation projects to improve efficiency and to ensure that facilities meet environmental, health, and security standards and comply with government regulations. Conduct classes to teach procedures to staff.

Employment Outlook: Employment of these workers is projected to increase as companies strive to maintain, secure, and efficiently operate their facilities. Competition should be keen for top managers; better opportunities are expected at the entry level.

Education of Workforce—Some College: 28.6%. **Associate Degree:** 12.2%. **Bachelor's Degree:** 27.5%. **Master's Degree:** 8.6%. **Doctorate/Professional Degree:** 1.6%. **Average Age:** 48. **Percentage of Women:** 32.6%.

Skills: Management of Financial Resources; Management of Material Resources; Management of Personnel Resources; Negotiation; Coordination; Time Management; Social Perceptiveness; Service Orientation. **Personality Type(s):** Enterprising-Conventional. **Work Environment:** Indoors; sitting.

Compensation and Benefits Managers

- Annual Earnings: $88,050
- Earnings Growth Potential: High
- Job Growth: 8.5%
- Annual Job Openings: 1,210
- Self-Employed: 0.6%

Plan, direct, or coordinate compensation and benefits activities and staff of an organization. Advise management on such matters as equal employment opportunity, sexual harassment, and discrimination. Direct preparation and distribution of written and verbal information to inform employees of benefits, compensation, and personnel policies. Administer, direct, and review employee benefit programs, including the integration of benefit programs following mergers and acquisitions. Plan and conduct new employee orientations to foster positive attitude toward organizational objectives. Identify and implement benefits to increase the quality of life for employees by working with brokers and researching benefits issues. Design, evaluate, and modify benefits policies to ensure that programs are current, competitive, and in compliance with legal requirements.

Employment Outlook: Efforts to recruit and retain employees, the growing importance of employee training, and new legal standards are expected to increase employment of these workers. College graduates and those with certification should have the best opportunities.

Education of Workforce—Some College: 21.7%. **Associate Degree:** 7.4%. **Bachelor's Degree:** 36.3%. **Master's Degree:** 17.8%. **Doctorate/Professional Degree:** 2.0%. **Average Age:** 45. **Percentage of Women:** No data available.

Skills: Management of Financial Resources; Operations Analysis; Systems Evaluation; Systems Analysis; Management of Personnel Resources; Time Management; Negotiation; Active Learning. **Personality Type(s):** Enterprising-Conventional-Social. **Work Environment:** Indoors; sitting.

Computer and Information Systems Managers

- Annual Earnings: $113,720

- Earnings Growth Potential: Medium

- Job Growth: 16.9%

- Annual Job Openings: 9,710

- Self-Employed: 3.3%

Plan, direct, or coordinate activities in such fields as electronic data processing, information systems, systems analysis, and computer programming. Manage backup, security, and user help systems. Consult with users, management, vendors, and technicians to assess computing needs and system requirements. Direct daily operations of department, analyzing workflow, establishing priorities, developing standards, and setting deadlines. Assign and review the work of systems analysts, programmers, and other computer-related workers. Stay abreast of advances in technology. Develop computer information resources, providing for data security and control, strategic computing, and disaster recovery. Review and approve all systems charts and programs prior to their implementation. Evaluate the organization's technology use and needs and recommend improvements, such as hardware and software upgrades. Control operational budget and expenditures. Meet with department heads, managers, supervisors, vendors, and others to solicit cooperation and resolve problems. Develop and interpret organizational goals, policies, and procedures.

Employment Outlook: New applications of technology in the workplace should continue to drive demand for IT services, fueling employment growth of these managers. Job prospects are expected to be excellent.

Education of Workforce—Some College: 15.7%. **Associate Degree:** 9.2%. **Bachelor's Degree:** 45.6%. **Master's Degree:** 22.2%. **Doctorate/ Professional Degree:** 2.2%. **Average Age:** 44. **Percentage of Women:** 27.2%.

Skills: Management of Financial Resources; Management of Material Resources; Programming; Systems Evaluation; Equipment Selection; Troubleshooting; Repairing; Technology Design. **Personality Type(s):** Enterprising-Conventional-Investigative. **Work Environment:** Indoors; sitting; using your hands to handle, control, or feel objects, tools, or controls.

Construction Managers

- Annual Earnings: $82,330
- Earnings Growth Potential: Medium
- Job Growth: 17.2%
- Annual Job Openings: 13,770
- Self-Employed: 60.9%

Plan, direct, coordinate, or budget, usually through subordinate supervisory personnel, activities concerned with the construction and maintenance of structures, facilities, and systems. Participate in the conceptual development of a construction project and oversee its organization, scheduling, and implementation. Confer with supervisory personnel, owners, contractors, and design professionals to discuss and resolve matters such as work procedures, complaints, and construction problems. Plan, organize, and direct activities concerned with the construction and maintenance of structures, facilities, and systems. Schedule the project in logical steps and budget time required to meet deadlines. Determine labor requirements and dispatch workers to construction sites. Inspect and review projects to monitor compliance with building and safety codes and other regulations. Interpret and explain plans and contract terms to administrative staff, workers, and clients, representing the owner or developer. Prepare contracts and negotiate revisions, changes, and additions to contractual agreements with architects, consultants, clients, suppliers, and subcontractors. Obtain all necessary permits and licenses. Direct and supervise workers. Study job specifications to determine appropriate construction methods.

Employment Outlook: As population and the number of businesses grow, building activity is expected to increase, which in turn will boost employment of construction managers. Prospects should be best for job seekers who have a bachelor's or higher degree in a construction-related discipline, plus construction experience.

Education of Workforce—Some College: 24.6%. **Associate Degree:** 8.1%. **Bachelor's Degree:** 23.2%. **Master's Degree:** 4.8%. **Doctorate/ Professional Degree:** 0.8%. **Average Age:** 46. **Percentage of Women:** 8.2%.

Skills: Management of Financial Resources; Management of Material Resources; Operations Analysis; Management of Personnel Resources; Mathematics; Negotiation; Persuasion; Systems Evaluation. **Personality Type(s):** Enterprising-Realistic-Conventional. **Work Environment:** More often outdoors than indoors; sounds, noisy; sitting; contaminants; hazardous equipment.

Crop and Livestock Managers

- Annual Earnings: $59,450

- Earnings Growth Potential: High

- Job Growth: 5.9%

- Annual Job Openings: 6,490

- Self-Employed: 0.0%

Job openings are shared with Aquacultural Managers and with Nursery and Greenhouse Managers.

Direct and coordinate, through subordinate supervisory personnel, activities of workers engaged in agricultural crop production for corporations, cooperatives, or other owners. Confer with buyers to arrange for the sale of crops. Record information such as production figures, farm management practices, and parent stock data and prepare financial and operational reports. Contract with farmers or independent owners for raising of crops or for management of crop production. Evaluate financial statements and make budget proposals. Analyze soil to determine types and quantities of fertilizer required for maximum production. Purchase machinery, equipment, and supplies, such as tractors, seed, fertilizer, and chemicals. Analyze market conditions to determine acreage allocations. Direct and coordinate worker activities such as planting, irrigation, chemical application, harvesting, and grading. Inspect orchards and fields to determine maturity dates of crops or to estimate potential crop damage from weather. Hire, discharge, transfer, and promote workers. Enforce applicable safety regulations. Negotiate with bank officials to obtain credit.

Employment Outlook: As farm productivity increases and consolidation continues, a decline in the number of farmers and ranchers is expected. Agricultural managers at larger, well-financed operations should have better prospects. Small, local farming offers the best entry-level opportunities.

Education of Workforce—Some College: 20.5%. **Associate Degree:** 8.5%. **Bachelor's Degree:** 21.4%. **Master's Degree:** 3.4%. **Doctorate/ Professional Degree:** 1.2%. **Average Age:** 50. **Percentage of Women:** 23.9%.

Skills: Management of Financial Resources; Management of Material Resources; Negotiation; Management of Personnel Resources; Operations Analysis; Systems Evaluation; Science; Systems Analysis. **Personality Type(s):** Enterprising-Realistic-Conventional. **Work Environment:** More often indoors than outdoors; sitting.

Financial Managers, Branch or Department

- Annual Earnings: $101,190

- Earnings Growth Potential: High

- Job Growth: 7.6%

- Annual Job Openings: 13,820

- Self-Employed: 5.3%

Job openings are shared with Treasurers and Controllers.

Direct and coordinate financial activities of workers in a branch, office, or department of an establishment, such as branch bank, brokerage firm, risk and insurance department, or credit department. Establish and maintain relationships with individual and business customers and provide assistance with problems these customers may encounter. Examine, evaluate, and process loan applications. Plan, direct, and coordinate the activities of workers in branches, offices, or departments of such establishments as branch banks, brokerage firms, risk and insurance departments, or credit departments. Oversee the flow of cash and financial instruments. Recruit staff members and oversee training programs. Network within communities to find and attract new business. Approve or reject, or coordinate the approval and rejection of, lines of credit and commercial, real estate, and personal loans. Prepare financial and regulatory reports required by laws, regulations, and boards of directors. Establish procedures for custody and control of assets, records, loan collateral, and securities in order to ensure safekeeping.

Employment Outlook: Business expansion and globalization will require financial expertise, which is expected to drive employment growth for these managers. Job growth, however, is expected to be tempered by mergers and downsizing. Keen competition is expected.

Education of Workforce—Some College: 19.5%. **Associate Degree:** 7.9%. **Bachelor's Degree:** 40.0%. **Master's Degree:** 17.1%. **Doctorate/ Professional Degree:** 2.1%. **Average Age:** 44. **Percentage of Women:** 54.8%.

Skills: Management of Financial Resources; Management of Personnel Resources; Persuasion; Service Orientation; Systems Evaluation; Learning Strategies; Time Management; Monitoring. **Personality Type(s):** Enterprising-Conventional. **Work Environment:** Indoors; sitting.

First-Line Supervisors/Managers of Construction Trades and Extraction Workers

- Annual Earnings: $58,330
- Earnings Growth Potential: Medium
- Job Growth: 15.4%
- Annual Job Openings: 24,220
- Self-Employed: 19.0%

Job openings are shared with Solar Energy Installation Managers.

Directly supervise and coordinate activities of construction or extraction workers. Examine and inspect work progress, equipment, and construction sites to verify safety and to ensure that specifications are met. Read specifications such as blueprints to determine construction requirements and to plan procedures. Estimate material and worker requirements to complete jobs. Supervise, coordinate, and schedule the activities of construction or extractive workers. Confer with managerial and technical personnel, other departments, and contractors in order to resolve problems and to coordinate activities. Coordinate work activities with other construction project activities. Order or requisition materials and supplies. Locate, measure, and mark site locations and placement of structures and equipment, using measuring and marking equipment. Record information such as personnel, production, and operational data on specified forms and reports. Assign work to employees, based on material and worker requirements of specific jobs.

Employment Outlook: Faster-than-average employment growth is projected.

Education of Workforce—Some College: 24.6%. **Associate Degree:** 6.6%. **Bachelor's Degree:** 8.8%. **Master's Degree:** 1.4%. **Doctorate/Professional Degree:** 0.4%. **Average Age:** 45. **Percentage of Women:** 2.7%.

Skills: Equipment Selection; Management of Personnel Resources; Operation and Control; Quality Control Analysis; Operations Analysis; Management of Material Resources; Troubleshooting; Operation Monitoring. **Personality Type(s):** Enterprising-Realistic-Conventional. **Work Environment:** Outdoors; sounds, noisy; very hot or cold temperatures; hazardous equipment; standing; contaminants.

First-Line Supervisors/Managers of Food Preparation and Serving Workers

- Annual Earnings: $29,470

- Earnings Growth Potential: Low

- Job Growth: 6.6%

- Annual Job Openings: 13,440

- Self-Employed: 3.2%

Supervise workers engaged in preparing and serving food. Compile and balance cash receipts at the end of the day or shift. Resolve customer complaints regarding food service. Train workers in food preparation and in service, sanitation, and safety procedures. Inspect supplies, equipment, and work areas to ensure efficient service and conformance to standards. Control inventories of food, equipment, smallware, and liquor and report shortages to designated personnel. Assign duties, responsibilities, and work stations to employees in accordance with work requirements. Estimate ingredients and supplies required to prepare a recipe. Analyze operational problems, such as theft and wastage, and establish procedures to alleviate these problems. Specify food portions and courses, production and time sequences, and workstation and equipment arrangements. Recommend measures for improving work procedures and worker performance to increase service quality and enhance job safety. Forecast staff, equipment, and supply requirements based on a master menu.

Employment Outlook: Consumer demand for convenience and a growing variety of dining venues are expected to create some jobs, but most openings are expected to arise from the need to replace workers who leave the occupation. Competition should be keen for jobs at upscale restaurants.

Education of Workforce—Some College: 25.9%. **Associate Degree:** 7.6%. **Bachelor's Degree:** 11.8%. **Master's Degree:** 1.5%. **Doctorate/ Professional Degree:** 0.5%. **Average Age:** 37. **Percentage of Women:** 57.8%.

Skills: Management of Financial Resources; Management of Material Resources; Systems Evaluation; Management of Personnel Resources; Coordination; Service Orientation; Time Management; Social Perceptiveness. **Personality Type(s):** Enterprising-Conventional-Realistic. **Work Environment:** Indoors; standing; walking and running; minor burns, cuts, bites, or stings; contaminants; making repetitive motions.

First-Line Supervisors/Managers of Logging Workers

- Annual Earnings: $40,500

- Earnings Growth Potential: High

- Job Growth: 7.8%

- Annual Job Openings: 1,630

- Self-Employed: 20.4%

Job openings are shared with Farm Labor Contractors, First-Line Supervisors/Managers of Agricultural Crop and Horticultural Workers, First-Line Supervisors/Managers of Animal Husbandry and Animal Care Workers, and First-Line Supervisors/Managers of Aquacultural Workers.

Directly supervise and coordinate activities of logging workers. Monitor workers to ensure that safety regulations are followed, warning or disciplining those who violate safety regulations. Plan and schedule logging operations such as felling and bucking trees and grading, sorting, yarding, or loading logs. Change logging operations or methods to eliminate unsafe conditions. Monitor logging operations to identify and solve problems; improve work methods; and ensure compliance with safety, company, and government regulations. Train workers in tree felling and bucking, operation of tractors and loading machines, yarding and loading techniques, and safety regulations. Determine logging operation methods, crew sizes, and equipment requirements, conferring with mill, company, and forestry officials as necessary. Assign to workers duties such as trees to be cut; cutting sequences and specifications; and loading of trucks, railcars, or rafts. Supervise and coordinate the activities of workers engaged in logging operations and silvicultural operations.

Employment Outlook: No data available.

Education of Workforce—Some College: 16.2%. **Associate Degree:** 5.1%. **Bachelor's Degree:** 11.3%. **Master's Degree:** 2.4%. **Doctorate/ Professional Degree:** 0.3%. **Average Age:** 47. **Percentage of Women:** No data available.

Skills: Operation and Control; Equipment Selection; Repairing; Equipment Maintenance; Management of Material Resources; Operation Monitoring; Troubleshooting; Management of Personnel Resources. **Personality Type(s):** Enterprising-Realistic-Conventional. **Work Environment:** Outdoors; hazardous equipment; minor burns, cuts, bites, or stings; sounds, noisy; very hot or cold temperatures; contaminants.

First-Line Supervisors/Managers of Mechanics, Installers, and Repairers

- Annual Earnings: $58,610

- Earnings Growth Potential: Medium

- Job Growth: 4.2%

- Annual Job Openings: 13,650

- Self-Employed: 0.4%

Supervise and coordinate the activities of mechanics, installers, and repairers. Determine schedules, sequences, and assignments for work activities, based on work priority, quantity of equipment, and skill of personnel. Monitor employees' work levels and review work performance. Monitor tool and part inventories and the condition and maintenance of shops to ensure adequate working conditions. Recommend or initiate personnel actions such as hires, promotions, transfers, discharges, and disciplinary measures. Investigate accidents and injuries, and prepare reports of findings. Compile operational and personnel records such as time and production records, inventory data, repair and maintenance statistics, and test results. Develop, implement, and evaluate maintenance policies and procedures. Counsel employees about work-related issues and assist employees to correct job-skill deficiencies. Examine objects, systems, or facilities, and analyze information to determine needed installations, services, or repairs.

Employment Outlook: Slower-than-average employment growth is projected.

Education of Workforce—Some College: 29.5%. **Associate Degree:** 11.9%. **Bachelor's Degree:** 10.0%. **Master's Degree:** 1.9%. **Doctorate/ Professional Degree:** 0.3%. **Average Age:** 46. **Percentage of Women:** 8.0%.

Skills: Repairing; Management of Financial Resources; Equipment Maintenance; Troubleshooting; Management of Material Resources; Equipment Selection; Quality Control Analysis; Operation and Control. **Personality Type(s):** Enterprising-Conventional-Realistic. **Work Environment:** More often indoors than outdoors; sounds, noisy; contaminants; hazardous conditions; standing.

First-Line Supervisors/Managers of Non-Retail Sales Workers

- Annual Earnings: $67,470

- Earnings Growth Potential: High

- Job Growth: 4.8%

- Annual Job Openings: 12,950

- Self-Employed: 45.6%

Directly supervise and coordinate activities of sales workers other than retail sales workers. May perform duties such as budgeting, accounting, and personnel work in addition to supervisory duties. Listen to and resolve customer complaints regarding services, products, or personnel. Monitor sales staff performance to ensure that goals are met. Hire, train, and evaluate personnel. Confer with company officials to develop methods and procedures to increase sales, expand markets, and promote business. Direct and supervise employees engaged in sales, inventory-taking, reconciling cash receipts, or performing specific services such as pumping gasoline for customers. Provide staff with assistance in performing difficult or complicated duties. Plan and prepare work schedules and assign employees to specific duties. Attend company meetings to exchange product information and coordinate work activities with other departments. Prepare sales and inventory reports for management and budget departments. Formulate pricing policies on merchandise according to profitability requirements. Examine merchandise to ensure correct pricing and display and ensure that it functions as advertised.

Employment Outlook: Limited job growth is expected as retailers increase the responsibilities of existing sales worker supervisors and as the retail industry grows slowly overall. Competition is expected. Job seekers with college degrees and retail experience should have the best prospects.

Education of Workforce—Some College: 23.7%. **Associate Degree:** 8.1%. **Bachelor's Degree:** 29.9%. **Master's Degree:** 7.5%. **Doctorate/ Professional Degree:** 1.4%. **Average Age:** 46. **Percentage of Women:** 26.1%.

Skills: Management of Financial Resources; Management of Material Resources; Systems Evaluation; Instructing; Negotiation; Management of Personnel Resources; Persuasion; Monitoring. **Personality Type(s):** Enterprising-Conventional-Social. **Work Environment:** Indoors; sounds, noisy.

First-Line Supervisors/Managers of Office and Administrative Support Workers

- Annual Earnings: $46,910
- Earnings Growth Potential: Medium
- Job Growth: 11.0%

- Annual Job Openings: 48,900

- Self-Employed: 1.4%

Supervise and coordinate the activities of clerical and administrative support workers. Resolve customer complaints and answer customers' questions regarding policies and procedures. Supervise the work of office, administrative, or customer service employees to ensure adherence to quality standards, deadlines, and proper procedures, correcting errors or problems. Provide employees with guidance in handling difficult or complex problems and in resolving escalated complaints or disputes. Implement corporate and departmental policies, procedures, and service standards in conjunction with management. Discuss job performance problems with employees to identify causes and issues and to work on resolving problems. Train and instruct employees in job duties and company policies or arrange for training to be provided. Evaluate employees' job performance and conformance to regulations and recommend appropriate personnel action. Recruit, interview, and select employees. Review records and reports pertaining to activities such as production, payroll, and shipping to verify details, monitor work activities, and evaluate performance. Interpret and communicate work procedures and company policies to staff. Prepare and issue work schedules, deadlines, and duty assignments of office or administrative staff. Maintain records pertaining to inventory, personnel, orders, supplies, and machine maintenance. Compute figures such as balances, totals, and commissions. Research, compile, and prepare reports, manuals, correspondence, and other information required by management or governmental agencies. Coordinate activities with other supervisory personnel and with other work units or departments. Analyze financial activities of establishments or departments and provide input into budget planning and preparation processes. Develop or update procedures, policies, and standards. Make recommendations to management concerning such issues as staffing decisions and procedural changes. Consult with managers and other personnel to resolve problems in areas such as equipment performance, output quality, and work schedules. Participate in the work of subordinates to facilitate productivity or to overcome difficult aspects of work.

Employment Outlook: Employment growth is expected to be tempered by technological advances that increase the productivity of—and thus decrease the need for—these workers and the workers they supervise. Keen competition is expected.

Education of Workforce—Some College: 30.5%. **Associate Degree:** 11.5%. **Bachelor's Degree:** 22.5%. **Master's Degree:** 5.5%. **Doctorate/ Professional Degree:** 1.1%. **Average Age:** 45. **Percentage of Women:** 71.2%.

Skills: Management of Financial Resources; Management of Material Resources; Negotiation; Monitoring; Management of Personnel Resources; Learning Strategies; Persuasion; Time Management. **Personality Type(s):** Enterprising-Conventional-Social. **Work Environment:** Indoors; sitting; sounds, noisy.

First-Line Supervisors/Managers of Production and Operating Workers

For job description, see Chapter 5.

First-Line Supervisors/Managers of Retail Sales Workers

- Annual Earnings: $34,900
- Earnings Growth Potential: Medium
- Job Growth: 5.2%
- Annual Job Openings: 45,010
- Self-Employed: 30.6%

Directly supervise sales workers in a retail establishment or department. Duties may include management functions, such as purchasing, budgeting, accounting, and personnel work, in addition to supervisory duties. Provide customer service by greeting and assisting customers and responding to customer inquiries and complaints. Direct and supervise employees engaged in sales, inventory-taking, reconciling cash receipts, or performing services for customers. Monitor sales activities to ensure that customers receive satisfactory service and quality goods. Inventory stock and reorder when inventory drops to a specified level. Instruct staff on how to handle difficult and complicated sales. Hire, train, and evaluate personnel in sales or marketing establishments, promoting or firing workers when appropriate. Assign employees to specific duties. Enforce safety, health, and security rules. Examine merchandise to ensure that it is correctly priced and displayed and that it functions as advertised. Plan budgets and authorize payments and merchandise returns. Perform work activities of subordinates, such as cleaning and organizing shelves and displays and selling merchandise.

Employment Outlook: Limited job growth is expected as retailers increase the responsibilities of existing sales worker supervisors and as the retail industry grows slowly overall. Competition is expected. Job seekers with college degrees and retail experience should have the best prospects.

Education of Workforce—Some College: 27.3%. **Associate Degree:** 8.8%. **Bachelor's Degree:** 20.7%. **Master's Degree:** 3.3%. **Doctorate/Professional Degree:** 0.7%. **Average Age:** 43. **Percentage of Women:** 43.3%.

Skills: Management of Financial Resources; Management of Material Resources; Negotiation; Management of Personnel Resources; Persuasion; Systems Evaluation; Learning Strategies; Instructing. **Personality Type(s):** Enterprising-Conventional-Social. **Work Environment:** Indoors; standing; walking and running; using your hands to handle, control, or feel objects, tools, or controls; making repetitive motions; sounds, noisy.

Food Service Managers

- Annual Earnings: $47,210

- Earnings Growth Potential: Medium

- Job Growth: 5.3%

- Annual Job Openings: 8,370

- Self-Employed: 42.0%

Plan, direct, or coordinate activities of an organization or department that serves food and beverages. Monitor compliance with health and fire regulations regarding food preparation and serving and building maintenance for lodging and dining facilities. Monitor food preparation methods, portion sizes, and garnishing and presentation of food to ensure that food is prepared and presented in an acceptable manner. Count money and make bank deposits. Investigate and resolve complaints regarding food quality, service, or accommodations. Coordinate assignments of cooking personnel to ensure economical use of food and timely preparation. Schedule and receive food and beverage deliveries, checking delivery contents to verify product quality and quantity. Monitor budgets and payroll records and review financial transactions to ensure that expenditures are authorized and budgeted. Schedule staff hours and assign duties. Maintain food and equipment inventories and keep inventory records. Establish standards for personnel performance and customer service.

Employment Outlook: Job losses resulting from a declining number of eating and drinking places will be partially offset by the creation of new jobs in grocery and convenience stores, health-care and elder-care facilities, and other establishments. Opportunities for new managers should be good because of the need to replace workers who leave the occupation.

Education of Workforce—Some College: 26.3%. **Associate Degree:** 8.7%. **Bachelor's Degree:** 20.3%. **Master's Degree:** 3.1%. **Doctorate/ Professional Degree:** 0.7%. **Average Age:** 42. **Percentage of Women:** 44.8%.

Skills: Management of Financial Resources; Management of Material Resources; Operations Analysis; Management of Personnel Resources; Negotiation; Service Orientation; Social Perceptiveness; Active Learning. **Personality Type(s):** Enterprising-Conventional-Realistic. **Work Environment:** Indoors; standing; walking and running; using your hands to handle, control, or feel objects, tools, or controls; making repetitive motions; sounds, noisy.

General and Operations Managers

- Annual Earnings: $92,650

- Earnings Growth Potential: High

- Job Growth: –0.1%

- Annual Job Openings: 50,220

- Self-Employed: 0.9%

Plan, direct, or coordinate the operations of companies or public- and private-sector organizations. Duties and responsibilities include formulating policies, managing daily operations, and planning the use of materials and human resources, but are too diverse and general in nature to be classified in any one functional area of management or administration, such as personnel, purchasing, or administrative services. Includes owners and managers who head small business establishments whose duties are primarily managerial. Direct and coordinate activities of businesses or departments concerned with the production, pricing, sales, or distribution of products. Manage staff, preparing work schedules and assigning specific duties. Review financial statements, sales and activity reports, and other performance data to measure productivity and goal achievement and to determine areas needing cost reduction and program improvement. Establish and implement departmental policies, goals, objectives, and procedures, conferring with board members, organization officials, and staff members as necessary. Determine staffing requirements and interview, hire, and train new employees or oversee those personnel processes. Monitor businesses and agencies to ensure that they efficiently and effectively provide needed services while staying within budgetary limits. Oversee activities directly related to making products or providing services.

Employment Outlook: The number of top executives is expected to remain steady, but employment may be adversely affected by consolidation and mergers. Keen competition is expected.

Education of Workforce—Some College: 23.9%. **Associate Degree:** 8.4%. **Bachelor's Degree:** 33.7%. **Master's Degree:** 12.4%. **Doctorate/ Professional Degree:** 2.4%. **Average Age:** 45. **Percentage of Women:** 30.1%.

Skills: Management of Material Resources; Management of Financial Resources; Operations Analysis; Management of Personnel Resources; Negotiation; Systems Analysis; Coordination; Systems Evaluation. **Personality Type(s):** Enterprising-Conventional-Social. **Work Environment:** Indoors; sitting; standing; sounds, noisy.

Human Resources Managers

- Annual Earnings: $92,244
- Earnings Growth Potential: Very high
- Job Growth: 9.6%
- Annual Job Openings: 4,140
- Self-Employed: 0.6%

Plan, direct, and coordinate human resource management activities of an organization to maximize the strategic use of human resources and maintain functions such as employee compensation, recruitment, personnel policies, and regulatory compliance. Administer compensation, benefits, and performance management systems and safety and recreation programs. Identify staff vacancies and recruit, interview, and select applicants. Allocate human resources, ensuring appropriate matches between personnel. Provide current and prospective employees with information about policies, job duties, working conditions, wages, opportunities for promotion, and employee benefits. Perform difficult staffing duties, including dealing with understaffing, refereeing disputes, firing employees, and administering disciplinary procedures. Advise managers on organizational policy matters such as equal employment opportunity and sexual harassment and recommend needed changes. Analyze and modify compensation and benefits policies to establish competitive programs and ensure compliance with legal requirements. Plan and conduct new employee orientation to foster positive attitude toward organizational objectives.

Employment Outlook: About-average employment growth is projected.

Education of Workforce—Some College: 21.7%. **Associate Degree:** 7.4%. **Bachelor's Degree:** 36.3%. **Master's Degree:** 17.8%. **Doctorate/ Professional Degree:** 2.0%. **Average Age:** 45. **Percentage of Women:** 66.3%.

Skills: Management of Financial Resources; Management of Personnel Resources; Management of Material Resources; Systems Evaluation; Negotiation; Systems Analysis; Persuasion; Learning Strategies. **Personality Type(s):** Enterprising-Social-Conventional. **Work Environment:** Indoors; sitting.

Management Analysts

For job description, see Chapter 5.

Marketing Managers

- Annual Earnings: $110,030
- Earnings Growth Potential: High
- Job Growth: 12.5%
- Annual Job Openings: 5,970
- Self-Employed: 4.1%

Determine the demand for products and services offered by firms and their competitors and identify potential customers. Develop pricing

strategies with the goal of maximizing firms' profits or shares of the market while ensuring that firms' customers are satisfied. Oversee product development or monitor trends that indicate the need for new products and services. Develop pricing strategies, balancing firm objectives and customer satisfaction. Identify, develop, and evaluate marketing strategy, based on knowledge of establishment objectives, market characteristics, and cost and markup factors. Evaluate the financial aspects of product development, such as budgets, expenditures, research and development appropriations, and return-on-investment and profit-loss projections. Formulate, direct, and coordinate marketing activities and policies to promote products and services, working with advertising and promotion managers. Direct the hiring, training, and performance evaluations of marketing and sales staff and oversee their daily activities. Negotiate contracts with vendors and distributors to manage product distribution, establishing distribution networks and developing distribution strategies. Compile lists describing product or service offerings.

Employment Outlook: Job growth is expected to result from companies' need to distinguish their products and services in an increasingly competitive marketplace. Keen competition is expected.

Education of Workforce—Some College: 17.6%. **Associate Degree:** 6.7%. **Bachelor's Degree:** 47.7%. **Master's Degree:** 16.6%. **Doctorate/ Professional Degree:** 1.4%. **Average Age:** 42. **Percentage of Women:** No data available.

Skills: Management of Financial Resources; Operations Analysis; Persuasion; Management of Material Resources; Negotiation; Systems Evaluation; Management of Personnel Resources; Systems Analysis. **Personality Type(s):** Enterprising-Conventional. **Work Environment:** Indoors; sitting.

Medical and Health Services Managers

- Annual Earnings: $81,850

- Earnings Growth Potential: Medium

- Job Growth: 16.0%

- Annual Job Openings: 9,940

- Self-Employed: 6.0%

Job openings are shared with Clinical Nurse Specialists.

Plan, direct, or coordinate medicine and health services in hospitals, clinics, managed care organizations, public health agencies, or similar organizations. Direct, supervise, and evaluate work activities of medical, nursing, technical, clerical, service, maintenance, and other personnel. Establish objectives and evaluative or operational criteria for units they manage. Direct or conduct recruitment, hiring, and training of personnel. Develop and maintain computerized record management systems to store and process data such as personnel activities and information and to produce reports. Develop and implement organizational policies and procedures for the facility or medical unit. Conduct and administer fiscal operations, including accounting, planning budgets, authorizing expenditures, establishing rates for services, and coordinating financial reporting. Establish work schedules and assignments for staff according to workload, space, and equipment availability. Maintain communication between governing boards, medical staff, and department heads by attending board meetings and coordinating interdepartmental functioning.

Employment Outlook: The health-care industry is expected to continue growing and diversifying, requiring managers increasingly to run business operations. Opportunities should be good, especially for job seekers who have work experience in health care and strong business management skills.

Education of Workforce—Some College: 16.1%. **Associate Degree:** 12.8%. **Bachelor's Degree:** 31.1%. **Master's Degree:** 22.5%. **Doctorate/ Professional Degree:** 7.1%. **Average Age:** 48. **Percentage of Women:** 69.4%.

Skills: Management of Financial Resources; Operations Analysis; Management of Material Resources; Science; Management of Personnel Resources; Systems Evaluation; Coordination; Time Management. **Personality Type(s):** Enterprising-Conventional-Social. **Work Environment:** Indoors; sitting; disease or infections.

Natural Sciences Managers

- Annual Earnings: $114,560
- Earnings Growth Potential: Medium
- Job Growth: 15.5%
- Annual Job Openings: 2,010
- Self-Employed: 0.0%

Job openings are shared with Clinical Research Coordinators and with Water Resource Specialists.

Plan, direct, or coordinate activities in such fields as life sciences, physical sciences, mathematics, and statistics and research and development in these fields. Confer with scientists, engineers, regulators, and others to plan and review projects and to provide technical assistance. Develop client relationships and communicate with clients to explain proposals, present research findings, establish specifications, or discuss project status. Plan and direct research, development, and production activities. Prepare project proposals. Design and coordinate successive phases of problem analysis, solution proposals, and testing. Review project activities and prepare and review research, testing, and operational reports. Hire, supervise, and evaluate engineers, technicians, researchers, and other staff. Determine scientific and technical goals within broad outlines provided by top management and make detailed plans to accomplish these goals. Develop and implement policies, standards, and procedures for the architectural, scientific, and technical work performed to ensure regulatory compliance and operations enhancement.

Employment Outlook: Employment is expected to grow along with that of the scientists and engineers these workers supervise. Prospects should be better in the rapidly growing areas of environmental and biomedical engineering and medical and environmental sciences.

Education of Workforce—Some College: 3.8%. **Associate Degree:** 1.3%. **Bachelor's Degree:** 33.3%. **Master's Degree:** 25.6%. **Doctorate/Professional Degree:** 33.9%. **Average Age:** 48. **Percentage of Women:** No data available.

Skills: Science; Operations Analysis; Management of Financial Resources; Technology Design; Management of Personnel Resources; Mathematics; Time Management; Reading Comprehension. **Personality Type(s):** Enterprising-Investigative. **Work Environment:** Indoors; sitting; sounds, noisy.

Property, Real Estate, and Community Association Managers

- Annual Earnings: $48,460

- Earnings Growth Potential: High

- Job Growth: 8.4%

- Annual Job Openings: 7,800

- Self-Employed: 45.9%

Plan, direct, or coordinate selling, buying, leasing, or governance activities of commercial, industrial, or residential real estate properties. Meet with prospective tenants to show properties, explain terms of occupancy, and provide information about local areas. Direct collection of monthly assessments; rental fees; and deposits and payment of insurance premiums, mortgage, taxes, and incurred operating expenses. Inspect grounds, facilities, and equipment routinely to determine necessity of repairs or maintenance. Investigate complaints, disturbances, and violations and resolve problems, following management rules and regulations. Manage and oversee operations, maintenance, administration, and improvement of commercial, industrial, or residential properties. Plan, schedule, and coordinate general maintenance, major repairs, and remodeling or construction projects for commercial or residential properties. Negotiate the sale, lease, or development of property and complete or review appropriate documents and forms.

Employment Outlook: Job growth is expected to be driven, in part, by a growing population and increasing use of third-party management companies for residential property oversight. Opportunities should be best for job seekers who have a college degree and earn professional designation.

Education of Workforce—Some College: 26.8%. **Associate Degree:** 8.2%. **Bachelor's Degree:** 28.1%. **Master's Degree:** 7.7%. **Doctorate/Professional Degree:** 2.3%. **Average Age:** 49. **Percentage of Women:** 49.6%.

Skills: Management of Financial Resources; Negotiation; Management of Personnel Resources; Persuasion; Operations Analysis; Management of Material Resources; Service Orientation; Writing. **Personality Type(s):** Enterprising-Conventional. **Work Environment:** More often indoors than outdoors; sitting.

Public Relations Managers

For job description, see Chapter 4.

Purchasing Managers

- Annual Earnings: $91,440
- Earnings Growth Potential: High
- Job Growth: 1.5%
- Annual Job Openings: 2,110
- Self-Employed: 3.6%

Plan, direct, or coordinate the activities of buyers, purchasing officers, and related workers involved in purchasing materials, products, and services. Represent companies in negotiating contracts and formulating policies with suppliers. Direct and coordinate activities of personnel engaged in buying, selling, and distributing materials, equipment, machinery, and supplies. Interview and hire staff and oversee staff training. Locate vendors of materials, equipment, or supplies and interview them to determine product availability and terms of sales. Prepare and process requisitions and purchase orders for supplies and equipment. Develop and implement purchasing and contract management instructions, policies, and procedures. Maintain records of goods ordered and received. Analyze market and delivery systems to assess present and future material availability. Participate in the development of specifications for equipment, products, or substitute materials. Resolve vendor or contractor grievances and claims against suppliers. Control purchasing department budgets. Review, evaluate, and approve specifications for issuing and awarding bids.

Employment Outlook: Almost all of the growth is expected to be for purchasing agents, except wholesale, retail, and farm products, as more companies demand a greater number of goods and services.

Education of Workforce—Some College: 21.7%. **Associate Degree:** 9.1%. **Bachelor's Degree:** 38.7%. **Master's Degree:** 15.4%. **Doctorate/ Professional Degree:** 2.2%. **Average Age:** 46. **Percentage of Women:** 40.4%.

Skills: Management of Financial Resources; Management of Material Resources; Negotiation; Management of Personnel Resources; Persuasion; Systems Evaluation; Systems Analysis; Coordination. **Personality Type(s):** Enterprising-Conventional. **Work Environment:** Indoors; sitting.

Quality Control Systems Managers

For job description, see Chapter 5.

Sales Managers

- Annual Earnings: $96,790

- Earnings Growth Potential: High

- Job Growth: 14.9%

- Annual Job Openings: 12,660

- Self-Employed: 4.2%

Direct the actual distribution or movement of products or services to customers. Coordinate sales distribution by establishing sales territories, quotas, and goals and establish training programs for sales representatives. Analyze sales statistics gathered by staff to determine sales potential and inventory requirements and monitor customer preferences. Resolve customer complaints regarding sales and service. Monitor customer preferences to determine focus of sales efforts. Direct and coordinate activities involving sales of manufactured products, services, commodities, real estate, or other subjects of sale. Determine price schedules and discount rates. Review operational records and reports to project sales and determine profitability. Direct, coordinate, and review activities in sales and service accounting and recordkeeping and in receiving and shipping operations. Confer or consult with department heads to plan advertising services and to secure information on equipment and customer specifications. Advise dealers and distributors on policies and operating procedures to ensure functional effectiveness of business. Prepare budgets and approve budget expenditures. Represent company at trade association meetings to promote products.

Employment Outlook: Job growth is expected to result from companies' need to distinguish their products and services in an increasingly competitive marketplace. Keen competition is expected.

Education of Workforce—Some College: 17.6%. **Associate Degree:** 6.7%. **Bachelor's Degree:** 47.7%. **Master's Degree:** 16.6%. **Doctorate/Professional Degree:** 1.4%. **Average Age:** 42. **Percentage of Women:** No data available.

Skills: Management of Financial Resources; Management of Personnel Resources; Management of Material Resources; Systems Evaluation; Persuasion; Monitoring; Negotiation; Systems Analysis. **Personality Type(s):** Enterprising-Conventional. **Work Environment:** Indoors; sitting.

Social and Community Service Managers

- Annual Earnings: $56,600

- Earnings Growth Potential: Medium

- Job Growth: 13.8%

- Annual Job Openings: 4,820

- Self-Employed: 3.1%

Plan, organize, or coordinate the activities of a social service program or community outreach organization. Oversee the program or organization's budget and policies regarding participant involvement, program requirements, and benefits. Work may involve directing social workers, counselors, or probation officers. Evaluate the work of staff and volunteers to ensure that programs are of appropriate quality and that resources are used effectively. Provide direct service and support to individuals or clients, such as handling a referral for child advocacy issues, conducting a needs evaluation, or resolving complaints. Recruit, interview, and hire or sign up volunteers and staff. Establish and maintain relationships with other agencies and organizations in community to meet community needs and to ensure that services are not duplicated. Establish and oversee administrative procedures to meet objectives set by boards of directors or senior management. Direct activities of professional and technical staff members and volunteers. Plan and administer budgets for programs, equipment, and support services. Participate in the determination of organizational policies regarding such issues as participant eligibility, program requirements, and program benefits.

Employment Outlook: Faster-than-average employment growth is projected.

Education of Workforce—Some College: 15.3%. **Associate Degree:** 6.3%. **Bachelor's Degree:** 37.7%. **Master's Degree:** 24.7%. **Doctorate/Professional Degree:** 4.9%. **Average Age:** 47. **Percentage of Women:** 68.1%.

Skills: Management of Financial Resources; Management of Personnel Resources; Management of Material Resources; Systems Evaluation; Operations Analysis; Social Perceptiveness; Systems Analysis; Learning Strategies. **Personality Type(s):** Enterprising-Social. **Work Environment:** Indoors; sitting.

CHAPTER 3

The Teaching Sequel

Don't believe the old saying, "Those who can't do, teach." Many people who leave another job and go into teaching *can* do. They decide to teach because they no longer want—or no longer have the opportunity—to "do." A teaching job may be worth considering as a sequel career.

What Teachers Do

From an early age, you have seen teachers at work. But maybe you've never thought much about what they were doing. Before they even set foot in a classroom, teachers need to organize a body of knowledge into a curriculum. To do this, they set learning goals (the broad purposes of the course) and objectives (measurable outcomes that demonstrate achievement of the goals). Then they have to communicate the body of knowledge in a way that's appropriate for the learners. Different people have different learning styles, and these can vary according to the age of the learner. Part of a teacher's challenge is using multiple teaching methods so nobody gets left behind. Some common strategies are reading assignments, lectures, discussions, teamwork, and hands-on work. Distance learning is growing in importance. Finally, teachers need to assess how much students have learned. You've sat through your share of tests, but you may not have thought about how difficult it is to design a test that fairly represents all the concepts and skills that the curriculum was supposed to impart. Instead, teachers sometimes have students create projects or portfolios to demonstrate their skills.

In the table at the end of Chapter 1, you saw the most prominent skills that O*NET lists for the teaching occupations. Now, also from O*NET, here are the most important **work activities** that you would do while teaching:

- Developing specific goals and plans to prioritize, organize, and accomplish your work.

- Identifying the educational needs of others, developing formal educational or training programs or classes, and teaching or instructing others.

- Keeping up to date technically and applying new knowledge to your job.

- Identifying the developmental needs of others and coaching, mentoring, or otherwise helping others to improve their knowledge or skills.

- Developing, designing, or creating new applications, ideas, relationships, systems, or products, including artistic contributions.

- Developing constructive and cooperative working relationships with others and maintaining them over time.

- Providing information to supervisors, co-workers, and subordinates by telephone, in written form, by e-mail, or in person.

- Analyzing information and evaluating results to choose the best solution and solve problems.

- Identifying information by categorizing, estimating, recognizing differences or similarities, and detecting changes in circumstances or events.

- Scheduling events, programs, and activities, as well as the work of others.

The Pros and Cons of Teaching

The common wisdom is that teachers are not high earners. However, because of their high level of education, teachers actually earn good incomes. The 42 teaching occupations surveyed by the Bureau of Labor Statistics earn an average of $50,867, compared to an average of $39,183 for all nonteaching occupations.

The BLS projects 19.2% growth for the teaching occupations from 2008 to 2018 and an average of 15,566 job openings per year.

The O*NET database reports these **work environment** characteristics for the teaching occupations:

- Indoors, Environmentally Controlled
- Freedom to Make Decisions
- Structured versus Unstructured Work
- Physical Proximity
- Frequency of Decision Making
- Impact of Decisions on Co-workers or Company Results
- Time Pressure
- Importance of Being Exact or Accurate
- Spend Time Standing
- Frequency of Conflict Situations

Like managers, teachers make many independent decisions and must live with the consequences of those decisions. The work environment can sometimes be stressful. On the other hand, many teachers enjoy the satisfaction of helping other people understand more and achieve more in life. Those who teach in public schools have more job security than workers in many other occupations.

How to Move into Teaching

Education goes on in many places, so there are many ways you can teach others the knowledge you have learned in your present job.

Some people who do this are vocational education teachers in public schools, commonly called *career and technical education (CTE) teachers* or *career-technology teachers.* If you were aiming for this as your first career choice, you would get a bachelor's degree in teacher education. That also is a good entry route if you don't have a bachelor's degree now. But if you're interested in teaching as a sequel career, your work experience in your previous job may allow you to get your foot in the classroom door without a bachelor's degree or teacher-education credits. In many states, you can get started teaching through this "alternate route," but usually you must immediately start completing the normal coursework in the evenings and summers so you can get a degree and pass the licensure exam.

Colleges and universities also employ many teachers. Usually you need at least a master's degree to teach there. To teach advanced courses, you generally need a doctoral degree and some track record of having done research. On the other hand, a community college that wants you to teach a hot career-related subject may not even require you to have a master's degree. Opportunities are much higher for part-time (adjunct) instructors than for full-timers, so this sequel career can be a good choice if you are looking for a way to ease into retirement.

Entry requirements are much looser if you want to teach your workplace skills in one of these settings:

- A career-oriented postsecondary school, such as a technical institute, a culinary arts school, a cosmetology school, or a business college.

- A corporate training center. Some businesses maintain an internal center, staffed with salaried trainers. Other businesses bring in outside contractors to train workers or use the services of an external training center.

- Seminars conducted at professional meetings or in hotels and other meeting places. The "lecture circuit" is one variation on this form of employment.

- Night classes where people study for self-enrichment. Some popular subjects are home repair, computer applications, and financial planning.

Not everyone has what it takes to be successful as a teacher. Technical knowledge alone is not enough. You need excellent communication skills, patience, the ability to think on your feet, and an easy acceptance of people with backgrounds and ages different from yours. The work can also be physically draining.

If you're interested in teaching in public schools, you should investigate nontraditional routes at the website of the National Center for Alternative Certification, www.teach-now.org.

For teaching at the postsecondary level, you can learn about employment opportunities in specialized publications on higher education, such as *The Chronicle of Higher Education*. The professional association in your field may also have information about academic jobs.

Most professional associations host lectures and workshops at their meetings. By volunteering for such presentations, you can get experience teaching work-related skills and develop a reputation in your industry. You can point to these experiences when you apply for a job at a postsecondary trade school or a corporate training company. For corporate training, it can be helpful to get certification from the American Society for Training and Development. Some other organizations certify trainers in specialized areas, such as computer technology.

One way to sample the work within your present job is to ask your manager to give you primary responsibility for training new workers at your immediate work site. If you show ability and remain interested in doing this, you may be able to take on the role of training workers elsewhere in the company or in the industry. For some fields, you may be able to teach a noncredit course at a local school or community organization. Tutoring one-on-one is yet another way to sample the teaching role and can turn into an income stream.

If your industry is declining, you may experience declining demand for people to train workers for it. In that case, once you have established a foothold in the teaching industry, you probably will want to change your focus and start teaching about topics for which demand is greater.

If your experiences have given you a message to convey that is especially valuable to know or emotionally uplifting, you may convince a speaker's bureau to represent you as a paid lecturer or motivational speaker.

If you're knowledgeable about a particular place and its history or natural environment, you may be able to lead narrated excursions for tourists.

Descriptions of Teaching Occupations

The teaching occupations in the O*NET database include 38 at the postsecondary level. That's too many to include in this book, so only 12, representing a wide variety of fields, are included among the 26 teaching occupations described here.

Adult Literacy, Remedial Education, and GED Teachers and Instructors

- Annual Earnings: $45,920

- Earnings Growth Potential: High

- Job Growth: 15.1%

- Annual Job Openings: 2,920

- Self-Employed: 20.4%

Teach or instruct out-of-school youths and adults in remedial education classes, preparatory classes for the General Educational Development test, literacy, or English as a Second Language. Teaching may or may not take place in a traditional educational institution. Adapt teaching methods and instructional materials to meet students' varying needs, abilities, and interests. Observe and evaluate students' work to determine progress and make suggestions for improvement. Plan and conduct activities for a balanced program of instruction, demonstration, and work time that provides students with opportunities to observe, question, and investigate. Instruct students individually and in groups, using various teaching methods such as lectures, discussions, and demonstrations. Maintain accurate and complete student records as required by laws or administrative policies. Prepare materials and classrooms for class activities. Establish clear objectives for all lessons, units, and projects and communicate those objectives to students. Conduct classes, workshops, and demonstrations to teach principles, techniques, or methods in subjects such as basic English language skills, life skills, and workforce entry skills.

Employment Outlook: As the need for educated workers increases, so will the need for teachers to instruct them. In addition, there should be employment growth for teachers to help immigrants and others improve their English language skills. Opportunities should be favorable.

Education of Workforce—Some College: 19.2%. **Associate Degree:** 8.0%. **Bachelor's Degree:** 35.0%. **Master's Degree:** 20.1%. **Doctorate/ Professional Degree:** 3.4%. **Average Age:** 42. **Percentage of Women:** No data available.

Skills: Learning Strategies; Instructing; Writing; Reading Comprehension; Persuasion; Time Management; Social Perceptiveness; Negotiation. **Personality Type(s):** Social-Artistic-Enterprising. **Work Environment:** Indoors; standing.

Agricultural Sciences Teachers, Postsecondary

- Annual Earnings: $77,210

- Earnings Growth Potential: High

- Job Growth: 15.1%

- Annual Job Openings: Roughly 300

- Self-Employed: 0.2%

Job openings are an estimated portion of those shared with 37 other postsecondary teaching occupations.

Teach courses in the agricultural sciences, including agronomy, dairy sciences, fisheries management, horticultural sciences, poultry sciences, range management, and agricultural soil conservation. Prepare course materials such as syllabi, homework assignments, and handouts. Evaluate and grade students' classwork, laboratory work, assignments, and papers. Keep abreast of developments in agriculture by reading current literature, talking with colleagues, and participating in professional conferences. Prepare and deliver lectures to undergraduate and/or graduate students on topics such as crop production, plant genetics, and soil chemistry. Initiate, facilitate, and moderate classroom discussions. Conduct research in a particular field of knowledge and publish findings in professional journals, books, and/or electronic media. Supervise laboratory sessions and fieldwork and coordinate laboratory operations. Supervise undergraduate and/or graduate teaching, internship, and research work. Compile, administer, and grade examinations or assign this work to others. Advise students on academic and vocational curricula and on career issues.

Employment Outlook: Enrollments in postsecondary institutions are expected to continue rising as more people attend college and as workers return to school to update their skills. Opportunities for part-time or temporary positions should be favorable, but significant competition exists for tenure-track positions.

Education of Workforce—Some College: 2.7%. **Associate Degree:** 2.3%. **Bachelor's Degree:** 15.3%. **Master's Degree:** 34.6%. **Doctorate/ Professional Degree:** 44.2%. **Average Age:** 45. **Percentage of Women:** No data available.

Skills: Instructing; Science; Writing; Speaking; Reading Comprehension; Active Learning; Learning Strategies; Operations Analysis. **Personality Type(s):** Social-Investigative-Realistic. **Work Environment:** Indoors; sitting.

Art, Drama, and Music Teachers, Postsecondary

- Annual Earnings: $60,400

- Earnings Growth Potential: High

- Job Growth: 15.1%

- Annual Job Openings: Roughly 2,500

- Self-Employed: 0.2%

Job openings are an estimated portion of those shared with 37 other postsecondary teaching occupations.

Teach courses in drama; music; and the arts, including fine and applied art, such as painting and sculpture, or design and crafts. Evaluate and grade students' classwork, performances, projects, assignments, and papers. Explain and demonstrate artistic techniques. Prepare students for performances, exams, or assessments. Prepare and deliver lectures to undergraduate or graduate students on topics such as acting techniques, fundamentals of music, and art history. Organize performance groups and direct their rehearsals. Prepare course materials such as syllabi, homework assignments, and handouts. Initiate, facilitate, and moderate classroom discussions. Keep abreast of developments in their field by reading current literature, talking with colleagues, and participating in professional conferences. Advise students on academic and vocational curricula and on career issues. Maintain student attendance records, grades, and other required records. Conduct research in a particular field of knowledge and publish findings in professional journals, books, or electronic media.

Employment Outlook: Enrollments in postsecondary institutions are expected to continue rising as more people attend college and as workers return to school to update their skills. Opportunities for part-time or temporary positions should be favorable, but significant competition exists for tenure-track positions.

Education of Workforce—Some College: 2.7%. **Associate Degree:** 2.3%. **Bachelor's Degree:** 15.3%. **Master's Degree:** 34.6%. **Doctorate/ Professional Degree:** 44.2%. **Average Age:** 45. **Percentage of Women:** No data available.

Skills: Instructing; Learning Strategies; Speaking; Reading Comprehension; Monitoring; Writing; Active Learning; Active Listening. **Personality Type(s):** Social-Artistic. **Work Environment:** Indoors; sitting; sounds, noisy.

Biological Science Teachers, Postsecondary

- Annual Earnings: $73,980
- Earnings Growth Potential: High
- Job Growth: 15.1%
- Annual Job Openings: Roughly 1,700
- Self-Employed: 0.2%

Job openings are an estimated portion of those shared with 37 other postsecondary teaching occupations.

Teach courses in biological sciences. Prepare and deliver lectures to undergraduate and/or graduate students on topics such as molecular biology, marine biology, and botany. Evaluate and grade students' classwork, laboratory work, assignments, and papers. Prepare course materials such as syllabi, homework assignments, and handouts. Compile, administer, and grade examinations or assign this work to others. Supervise students' laboratory work. Keep abreast of developments in their field by reading current literature, talking with colleagues, and participating in professional conferences. Maintain student attendance records, grades, and other required records. Initiate, facilitate, and moderate classroom discussions. Plan, evaluate, and revise curricula, course content, course materials, and methods of instruction. Advise students on academic and vocational curricula and on career issues. Maintain regularly scheduled office hours to advise and assist students.

Employment Outlook: Enrollments in postsecondary institutions are expected to continue rising as more people attend college and as workers return to school to update their skills. Opportunities for part-time or temporary positions should be favorable, but significant competition exists for tenure-track positions.

Education of Workforce—Some College: 2.7%. **Associate Degree:** 2.3%. **Bachelor's Degree:** 15.3%. **Master's Degree:** 34.6%. **Doctorate/ Professional Degree:** 44.2%. **Average Age:** 45. **Percentage of Women:** No data available.

Skills: Science; Instructing; Writing; Speaking; Learning Strategies; Reading Comprehension; Active Learning; Operations Analysis. **Personality Type(s):** Social-Investigative. **Work Environment:** Indoors; sitting; standing.

Business Teachers, Postsecondary

- Annual Earnings: $73,320

- Earnings Growth Potential: Very high

- Job Growth: 15.1%

- Annual Job Openings: Roughly 2,000

- Self-Employed: 0.2%

Job openings are an estimated portion of those shared with 37 other postsecondary teaching occupations.

Teach courses in business administration and management, such as accounting, finance, human resources, labor relations, marketing, and operations research. Prepare and deliver lectures to undergraduate and/ or graduate students on topics such as financial accounting, principles of marketing, and operations management. Evaluate and grade students' classwork, assignments, and papers. Compile, administer, and grade examinations or assign this work to others. Prepare course materials such as syllabi, homework assignments, and handouts. Maintain student attendance records, grades, and other required records. Initiate, facilitate, and moderate classroom discussions. Plan, evaluate, and revise curricula, course content, and course materials and methods of instruction. Keep abreast of developments in their field by reading current literature, talking with colleagues, and participating in professional organizations and conferences. Maintain regularly scheduled office hours to advise and assist students. Advise students on academic and vocational curricula and on career issues. Select and obtain materials and supplies such as textbooks.

Employment Outlook: Enrollments in postsecondary institutions are expected to continue rising as more people attend college and as workers return to school to update their skills. Opportunities for part-time or temporary positions should be favorable, but significant competition exists for tenure-track positions.

Education of Workforce—Some College: 2.7%. **Associate Degree:** 2.3%. **Bachelor's Degree:** 15.3%. **Master's Degree:** 34.6%. **Doctorate/ Professional Degree:** 44.2%. **Average Age:** 45. **Percentage of Women:** No data available.

Skills: Learning Strategies; Instructing; Reading Comprehension; Writing; Active Learning; Speaking; Judgment and Decision Making; Systems Analysis. **Personality Type(s):** Social-Enterprising-Investigative. **Work Environment:** Indoors; sitting.

Chemistry Teachers, Postsecondary

- Annual Earnings: $68,760

- Earnings Growth Potential: High

- Job Growth: 15.1%

- Annual Job Openings: Roughly 600

- Self-Employed: 0.2%

Job openings are an estimated portion of those shared with 37 other postsecondary teaching occupations.

Teach courses pertaining to the chemical and physical properties and compositional changes of substances. Work may include instruction in the methods of qualitative and quantitative chemical analysis. Includes both teachers primarily engaged in teaching and those who do a combination of both teaching and research. Prepare and deliver lectures to undergraduate and/or graduate students on topics such as organic chemistry, analytical chemistry, and chemical separation. Supervise students' laboratory work. Evaluate and grade students' classwork, laboratory performance, assignments, and papers. Compile, administer, and grade examinations or assign this work to others. Maintain student attendance records, grades, and other required records. Prepare course materials such as syllabi, homework assignments, and handouts. Maintain regularly scheduled office hours to advise and assist students. Plan, evaluate, and revise curricula, course content, course materials, and methods of instruction. Supervise undergraduate and/or graduate teaching, internships, and research work. Keep abreast of developments in the field by reading current literature, talking with colleagues, and participating in professional conferences. Initiate, facilitate, and moderate classroom discussions.

Employment Outlook: Enrollments in postsecondary institutions are expected to continue rising as more people attend college and as workers return to school to update their skills. Opportunities for part-time or temporary positions should be favorable, but significant competition exists for tenure-track positions.

Education of Workforce—Some College: 2.7%. **Associate Degree:** 2.3%. **Bachelor's Degree:** 15.3%. **Master's Degree:** 34.6%. **Doctorate/ Professional Degree:** 44.2%. **Average Age:** 45. **Percentage of Women:** No data available.

Skills: Science; Reading Comprehension; Speaking; Writing; Learning Strategies; Instructing; Operations Analysis; Active Learning. **Personality Type(s):** Social-Investigative-Realistic. **Work Environment:** Indoors; hazardous conditions; contaminants; sitting.

Computer Science Teachers, Postsecondary

- Annual Earnings: $68,580

- Earnings Growth Potential: High

- Job Growth: 15.1%

- Annual Job Openings: Roughly 1,000

- Self-Employed: 0.2%

Job openings are an estimated portion of those shared with 37 other postsecondary teaching occupations.

Teach courses in computer science. May specialize in a field of computer science, such as the design and function of computers or operations and research analysis. Evaluate and grade students' classwork, laboratory work, assignments, and papers. Maintain student attendance records, grades, and other required records. Prepare and deliver lectures to undergraduate and/or graduate students on topics such as programming, data structures, and software design. Prepare course materials such as syllabi, homework assignments, and handouts. Compile, administer, and grade examinations or assign this work to others. Keep abreast of developments in their field by reading current literature, talking with colleagues, and participating in professional conferences. Initiate, facilitate, and moderate classroom discussions. Plan, evaluate, and revise curricula, course content, and course materials and methods of instruction. Supervise students' laboratory work. Maintain regularly scheduled office hours to advise and assist students. Select and obtain materials and supplies such as textbooks and laboratory equipment.

Employment Outlook: Enrollments in postsecondary institutions are expected to continue rising as more people attend college and as workers return to school to update their skills. Opportunities for part-time or temporary positions should be favorable, but significant competition exists for tenure-track positions.

Education of Workforce—Some College: 2.7%. **Associate Degree:** 2.3%. **Bachelor's Degree:** 15.3%. **Master's Degree:** 34.6%. **Doctorate/ Professional Degree:** 44.2%. **Average Age:** 45. **Percentage of Women:** No data available.

Skills: Programming; Writing; Learning Strategies; Instructing; Reading Comprehension; Active Learning; Speaking; Systems Analysis. **Personality Type(s):** Social-Investigative-Conventional. **Work Environment:** Indoors; sitting.

Criminal Justice and Law Enforcement Teachers, Postsecondary

- Annual Earnings: $57,500

- Earnings Growth Potential: High

- Job Growth: 15.1%

- Annual Job Openings: Roughly 400

- Self-Employed: 0.2%

Job openings are an estimated portion of those shared with 37 other postsecondary teaching occupations.

Teach courses in criminal justice, corrections, and law enforcement administration. Initiate, facilitate, and moderate classroom discussions. Keep abreast of developments in their field by reading current literature, talking with colleagues, and participating in professional conferences. Evaluate and grade students' classwork, assignments, and papers. Compile, administer, and grade examinations or assign this work to others. Prepare and deliver lectures to undergraduate or graduate students on topics such as criminal law, defensive policing, and investigation techniques. Prepare course materials such as syllabi, homework assignments, and handouts. Conduct research in a particular field of knowledge and publish findings in professional journals, books, and/or electronic media. Plan, evaluate, and revise curricula, course content, and course materials and methods of instruction. Supervise undergraduate and/or graduate teaching, internship, and research work. Maintain student attendance records, grades, and other required records.

Employment Outlook: Enrollments in postsecondary institutions are expected to continue rising as more people attend college and as workers return to school to update their skills. Opportunities for part-time or temporary positions should be favorable, but significant competition exists for tenure-track positions.

Education of Workforce—Some College: 2.7%. **Associate Degree:** 2.3%. **Bachelor's Degree:** 15.3%. **Master's Degree:** 34.6%. **Doctorate/ Professional Degree:** 44.2%. **Average Age:** 45. **Percentage of Women:** No data available.

Skills: Writing; Learning Strategies; Speaking; Reading Comprehension; Instructing; Active Listening; Active Learning; Systems Analysis. **Personality Type(s):** Social-Investigative. **Work Environment:** Indoors; sitting.

Elementary School Teachers, Except Special Education

- Annual Earnings: $50,510

- Earnings Growth Potential: Low

- Job Growth: 15.8%

- Annual Job Openings: 59,650

- Self-Employed: 0.0%

Teach pupils in public or private schools at the elementary level basic academic, social, and other formative skills. Establish and enforce rules for behavior and procedures for maintaining order among the students for whom they are responsible. Observe and evaluate students' performance, behavior, social development, and physical health. Prepare materials and classrooms for class activities. Adapt teaching methods and instructional materials to meet students' varying needs and interests. Plan and conduct activities for a balanced program of instruction, demonstration, and work time that provides students with opportunities to observe, question, and investigate. Instruct students individually and in groups, using various teaching methods such as lectures, discussions, and demonstrations. Establish clear objectives for all lessons, units, and projects and communicate those objectives to students. Assign and grade classwork and homework. Read books to entire classes or small groups. Prepare, administer, and grade tests and assignments to evaluate students' progress.

Employment Outlook: Enrollment over the projections decade is expected to grow more slowly than in recent years. Prospects are usually better in urban and rural areas, for bilingual teachers, and for math and science teachers.

Education of Workforce—Some College: 2.9%. **Associate Degree:** 2.1%. **Bachelor's Degree:** 46.5%. **Master's Degree:** 44.4%. **Doctorate/ Professional Degree:** 2.9%. **Average Age:** 43. **Percentage of Women:** No data available.

Skills: Learning Strategies; Social Perceptiveness; Systems Evaluation; Monitoring; Service Orientation; Writing; Systems Analysis; Instructing. **Personality Type(s):** Social-Artistic-Conventional. **Work Environment:** Indoors; standing; sounds, noisy.

Engineering Teachers, Postsecondary

- Annual Earnings: $85,830
- Earnings Growth Potential: High
- Job Growth: 15.1%
- Annual Job Openings: Roughly 1,000
- Self-Employed: 0.2%

Job openings are an estimated portion of those shared with 37 other postsecondary teaching occupations.

Teach courses pertaining to the application of physical laws and principles of engineering for the development of machines, materials, instruments, processes, and services. Includes teachers of subjects such as chemical, civil, electrical, industrial, mechanical, mineral, and petroleum engineering. Includes both teachers primarily engaged in teaching and those who do a combination of both teaching and research. Prepare and deliver lectures to undergraduate and/or graduate students on topics such as mechanics, hydraulics, and robotics. Keep abreast of developments in their field by reading current literature, talking with colleagues, and participating in professional conferences. Supervise undergraduate and/ or graduate teaching, internship, and research work. Evaluate and grade students' classwork, laboratory work, assignments, and papers. Conduct research in a particular field of knowledge and publish findings in professional journals, books, and/or electronic media. Prepare course materials such as syllabi, homework assignments, and handouts. Compile, administer, and grade examinations or assign this work to others. Write grant proposals to procure external research funding. Supervise students' laboratory work. Initiate, facilitate, and moderate class discussions. Maintain regularly scheduled office hours to advise and assist students.

Employment Outlook: Enrollments in postsecondary institutions are expected to continue rising as more people attend college and as workers return to school to update their skills. Opportunities for part-time or temporary positions should be favorable, but significant competition exists for tenure-track positions.

Education of Workforce—Some College: 2.7%. **Associate Degree:** 2.3%. **Bachelor's Degree:** 15.3%. **Master's Degree:** 34.6%. **Doctorate/Professional Degree:** 44.2%. **Average Age:** 45. **Percentage of Women:** No data available.

Skills: Instructing; Mathematics; Operations Analysis; Science; Writing; Speaking; Reading Comprehension; Active Learning. **Personality Type(s):** Investigative-Realistic-Social. **Work Environment:** Indoors; sitting.

Farm and Home Management Advisors

- Annual Earnings: $44,180

- Earnings Growth Potential: High

- Job Growth: 1.1%

- Annual Job Openings: 300

- Self-Employed: 2.6%

Advise, instruct, and assist individuals and families engaged in agriculture, agricultural-related processes, or home economics activities. Demonstrate procedures and apply research findings to solve problems; instruct and train in product development, sales, and the utilization of machinery and equipment to promote general welfare. Includes county agricultural agents, feed and farm management advisers, home economists, and extension service advisors. Collaborate with producers in order to diagnose and prevent management and production problems. Conduct classes or deliver lectures on subjects such as nutrition, home management, and farming techniques. Advise farmers and demonstrate techniques in areas such as feeding and health maintenance of livestock, growing and harvesting practices, and financial planning. Research information requested by farmers. Prepare and distribute leaflets, pamphlets, and visual aids for educational and informational purposes. Collect and evaluate data in order to determine community program needs. Maintain records of services provided and the effects of advice given. Schedule and make regular visits to farmers. Organize, advise, and participate in community activities and organizations such as county and state fair events and 4-H Clubs.

Employment Outlook: Little or no employment change is projected.

Education of Workforce—Some College: 10.3%. **Associate Degree:** 5.5%. **Bachelor's Degree:** 25.4%. **Master's Degree:** 44.5%. **Doctorate/ Professional Degree:** 8.1%. **Average Age:** 47. **Percentage of Women:** No data available.

Skills: Learning Strategies; Systems Evaluation; Active Learning; Systems Analysis; Science; Management of Financial Resources; Mathematics; Instructing. **Personality Type(s):** Social-Realistic-Enterprising. **Work Environment:** Indoors; sitting.

Health Educators

- Annual Earnings: $44,340

- Earnings Growth Potential: High

- Job Growth: 18.2%

- Annual Job Openings: 2,600

- Self-Employed: 0.3%

Promote, maintain, and improve individual and community health by assisting individuals and communities to adopt healthy behaviors. Collect and analyze data to identify community needs prior to planning, implementing, monitoring, and evaluating programs designed to encourage healthy lifestyles, policies, and environments. May also serve as a resource to assist individuals, other professionals, or the community and may administer fiscal resources for health education programs. Document activities, recording information such as the numbers of applications completed, presentations conducted, and persons assisted. Develop and present health education and promotion programs such as training workshops, conferences, and school or community presentations. Develop and maintain cooperative working relationships with agencies and organizations interested in public health care. Prepare and distribute health education materials, including reports; bulletins; and visual aids such as films, videotapes, photographs, and posters. Develop operational plans and policies necessary to achieve health education objectives and services.

Collaborate with health specialists and civic groups to determine community health needs and the availability of services and to develop goals for meeting needs. Maintain databases, mailing lists, telephone networks, and other information to facilitate the functioning of health education programs.

Employment Outlook: As health-care costs rise, insurance companies, businesses, and governments are expected to hire health educators to teach the public how to avoid and detect illnesses. Opportunities should be favorable, especially for those who have gained experience through volunteer work or internships.

Education of Workforce—Some College: 20.9%. **Associate Degree:** 9.6%. **Bachelor's Degree:** 37.1%. **Master's Degree:** 13.4%. **Doctorate/Professional Degree:** 1.3%. **Average Age:** 42. **Percentage of Women:** No data available.

Skills: Operations Analysis; Science; Writing; Learning Strategies; Speaking; Persuasion; Social Perceptiveness; Service Orientation. **Personality Type(s):** Social-Enterprising. **Work Environment:** Indoors; using your hands to handle, control, or feel objects, tools, or controls; disease or infections; sitting.

Health Specialties Teachers, Postsecondary

- Annual Earnings: $84,840

- Earnings Growth Potential: Very high

- Job Growth: 15.1%

- Annual Job Openings: Roughly 4,000

- Self-Employed: 0.2%

Job openings are an estimated portion of those shared with 37 other postsecondary teaching occupations.

Teach courses in health specialties, such as veterinary medicine, dentistry, pharmacy, therapy, laboratory technology, and public health. Initiate, facilitate, and moderate classroom discussions. Keep abreast of developments in their field by reading current literature, talking with colleagues, and participating in professional conferences. Compile, administer, and grade examinations or assign this work to others. Evaluate and grade students' classwork, assignments, and papers. Prepare course materials such as syllabi, homework assignments, and handouts. Prepare and deliver lectures to undergraduate or graduate students on topics such as public health, stress management, and worksite health promotion. Plan, evaluate, and revise curricula, course content, and course materials and methods of instruction. Supervise undergraduate or graduate teaching, internship, and research work. Conduct research in a particular field of knowledge and publish findings in professional journals, books, or electronic media. Collaborate with colleagues to address teaching and research issues. Supervise laboratory sessions.

Employment Outlook: Enrollments in postsecondary institutions are expected to continue rising as more people attend college and as workers return to school to update their skills. Opportunities for part-time or temporary positions should be favorable, but significant competition exists for tenure-track positions.

Education of Workforce—Some College: 2.7%. **Associate Degree:** 2.3%. **Bachelor's Degree:** 15.3%. **Master's Degree:** 34.6%. **Doctorate/ Professional Degree:** 44.2%. **Average Age:** 45. **Percentage of Women:** No data available.

Skills: Instructing; Learning Strategies; Reading Comprehension; Writing; Science; Active Learning; Speaking; Active Listening. **Personality Type(s):** Social-Investigative. **Work Environment:** Indoors; sitting.

Mathematical Science Teachers, Postsecondary

- Annual Earnings: $63,640

- Earnings Growth Potential: High

- Job Growth: 15.1%

- Annual Job Openings: Roughly 1,000

- Self-Employed: 0.2%

Job openings are an estimated portion of those shared with 37 other postsecondary teaching occupations.

Teach courses pertaining to mathematical concepts, statistics, and actuarial science and to the application of original and standardized mathematical techniques in solving specific problems and situations.

Evaluate and grade students' classwork, assignments, and papers. Compile, administer, and grade examinations or assign this work to others. Prepare and deliver lectures to undergraduate and/or graduate students on topics such as linear algebra, differential equations, and discrete mathematics. Prepare course materials such as syllabi, homework assignments, and handouts. Maintain student attendance records, grades, and other required records. Maintain regularly scheduled office hours to advise and assist students. Plan, evaluate, and revise curricula, course content, and course materials and methods of instruction. Initiate, facilitate, and moderate classroom discussions. Select and obtain materials and supplies such as textbooks. Keep abreast of developments in their field by reading current literature, talking with colleagues, and participating in professional conferences. Advise students on academic and vocational curricula and on career issues.

Employment Outlook: Enrollments in postsecondary institutions are expected to continue rising as more people attend college and as workers return to school to update their skills. Opportunities for part-time or temporary positions should be favorable, but significant competition exists for tenure-track positions.

Education of Workforce—Some College: 2.7%. **Associate Degree:** 2.3%. **Bachelor's Degree:** 15.3%. **Master's Degree:** 34.6%. **Doctorate/ Professional Degree:** 44.2%. **Average Age:** 45. **Percentage of Women:** No data available.

Skills: Mathematics; Writing; Learning Strategies; Instructing; Reading Comprehension; Systems Evaluation; Active Learning; Speaking. **Personality Type(s):** Social-Investigative-Artistic. **Work Environment:** Indoors; standing; sitting.

Middle School Teachers, Except Special and Vocational Education

- Annual Earnings: $50,770
- Earnings Growth Potential: Low
- Job Growth: 15.3%
- Annual Job Openings: 25,110
- Self-Employed: 0.0%

Teach students in public or private schools in one or more subjects at the middle, intermediate, or junior high level, which falls between

elementary and senior high school as defined by applicable state laws and regulations. Establish and enforce rules for behavior and procedures for maintaining order among students. Adapt teaching methods and instructional materials to meet students' varying needs and interests. Instruct through lectures, discussions, and demonstrations in one or more subjects, such as English, mathematics, or social studies. Prepare, administer, and grade tests and assignments to evaluate students' progress. Establish clear objectives for all lessons, units, and projects and communicate these objectives to students. Plan and conduct activities for a balanced program of instruction, demonstration, and work time that provides students with opportunities to observe, question, and investigate. Maintain accurate, complete, and correct student records as required by laws, district policies, and administrative regulations. Observe and evaluate students' performance, behavior, social development, and physical health. Prepare materials and classrooms for class activities.

Employment Outlook: Enrollment over the projections decade is expected to grow more slowly than in recent years. Prospects are usually better in urban and rural areas, for bilingual teachers, and for math and science teachers.

Education of Workforce—Some College: 2.9%. **Associate Degree:** 2.1%. **Bachelor's Degree:** 46.5%. **Master's Degree:** 44.4%. **Doctorate/ Professional Degree:** 2.9%. **Average Age:** 43. **Percentage of Women:** 81.2%.

Skills: Learning Strategies; Instructing; Negotiation; Writing; Social Perceptiveness; Reading Comprehension; Active Listening; Systems Evaluation. **Personality Type(s):** Social-Artistic. **Work Environment:** Indoors; standing; sounds, noisy.

Nursing Instructors and Teachers, Postsecondary

- Annual Earnings: $61,360

- Earnings Growth Potential: Medium

- Job Growth: 15.1%

- Annual Job Openings: Roughly 1,500

- Self-Employed: 0.2%

Job openings are an estimated portion of those shared with 37 other postsecondary teaching occupations.

Demonstrate and teach patient care in classroom and clinical units to nursing students. Includes both teachers primarily engaged in teaching and those who do a combination of both teaching and research. Initiate, facilitate, and moderate classroom discussions. Prepare and deliver lectures to undergraduate or graduate students on topics such as pharmacology, mental health nursing, and community health-care practices. Keep abreast of developments in their field by reading current literature, talking with colleagues, and participating in professional conferences. Prepare course materials such as syllabi, homework assignments, and handouts. Supervise students' laboratory and clinical work. Evaluate and grade students' classwork, laboratory and clinic work, assignments, and papers. Collaborate with colleagues to address teaching and research issues. Plan, evaluate, and revise curricula, course content, and course materials and methods of instruction. Assess clinical education needs and patient and client teaching needs, utilizing a variety of methods. Compile, administer, and grade examinations or assign this work to others.

Employment Outlook: Enrollments in postsecondary institutions are expected to continue rising as more people attend college and as workers return to school to update their skills. Opportunities for part-time or temporary positions should be favorable, but significant competition exists for tenure-track positions.

Education of Workforce—Some College: 2.7%. **Associate Degree:** 2.3%. **Bachelor's Degree:** 15.3%. **Master's Degree:** 34.6%. **Doctorate/ Professional Degree:** 44.2%. **Average Age:** 45. **Percentage of Women:** No data available.

Skills: Instructing; Science; Writing; Learning Strategies; Speaking; Reading Comprehension; Active Learning; Active Listening. **Personality Type(s):** Social-Investigative. **Work Environment:** Indoors; disease or infections; sitting.

Secondary School Teachers, Except Special and Vocational Education

- Annual Earnings: $52,200
- Earnings Growth Potential: Low
- Job Growth: 8.9%
- Annual Job Openings: 41,240
- Self-Employed: 0.0%

Instruct students in secondary public or private schools in one or more subjects at the secondary level, such as English, mathematics, or social studies. May be designated according to subject matter specialty, such as typing instructors, commercial teachers, or English teachers. Establish and enforce rules for behavior and procedures for maintaining order among students. Instruct through lectures, discussions, and demonstrations in one or more subjects, such as English, mathematics, or social studies. Establish clear objectives for all lessons, units, and projects and communicate those objectives to students. Prepare, administer, and grade tests and assignments to evaluate students' progress. Prepare materials and classrooms for class activities. Adapt teaching methods and instructional materials to meet students' varying needs and interests. Maintain accurate and complete student records as required by laws, district policies, and administrative regulations. Assign and grade classwork and homework. Observe and evaluate students' performance, behavior, social development, and physical health. Enforce all administration policies and rules governing students.

Employment Outlook: Enrollment over the projections decade is expected to grow more slowly than in recent years. Prospects are usually better in urban and rural areas, for bilingual teachers, and for math and science teachers.

Education of Workforce—Some College: 2.3%. **Associate Degree:** 1.6%. **Bachelor's Degree:** 45.3%. **Master's Degree:** 46.5%. **Doctorate/ Professional Degree:** 3.3%. **Average Age:** 43. **Percentage of Women:** 56.0%.

Skills: Learning Strategies; Systems Evaluation; Instructing; Social Perceptiveness; Service Orientation; Writing; Speaking; Judgment and Decision Making. **Personality Type(s):** Social-Artistic-Enterprising. **Work Environment:** Indoors; standing.

Self-Enrichment Education Teachers

- Annual Earnings: $36,440
- Earnings Growth Potential: High
- Job Growth: 32.0%
- Annual Job Openings: 12,030
- Self-Employed: 17.3%

Teach or instruct courses other than those that normally lead to an occupational objective or degree. Courses may include self-improvement, nonvocational, and nonacademic subjects. Teaching may or may not take place in a traditional educational institution. Adapt teaching methods and instructional materials to meet students' varying needs and interests. Conduct classes, workshops, and demonstrations and provide individual instruction to teach topics and skills such as cooking, dancing, writing, physical fitness, photography, personal finance, and flying. Monitor students' performance to make suggestions for improvement and to ensure that they satisfy course standards, training requirements, and objectives. Observe students to determine qualifications, limitations, abilities, interests, and other individual characteristics. Instruct students individually and in groups, using various teaching methods such as lectures, discussions, and demonstrations. Establish clear objectives for all lessons, units, and projects and communicate those objectives to students. Instruct and monitor students in use and care of equipment and materials to prevent injury and damage.

Employment Outlook: Demand for self-enrichment education will increase as more people embrace lifelong learning or seek to acquire or improve skills that make them more attractive to prospective employers. Opportunities should be favorable.

Education of Workforce—Some College: 19.2%. **Associate Degree:** 8.0%. **Bachelor's Degree:** 35.0%. **Master's Degree:** 20.1%. **Doctorate/ Professional Degree:** 3.4%. **Average Age:** 42. **Percentage of Women:** No data available.

Skills: Operations Analysis; Learning Strategies; Instructing; Persuasion; Active Learning; Speaking; Repairing; Troubleshooting. **Personality Type(s):** Social-Artistic-Enterprising. **Work Environment:** Indoors; standing.

Special Education Teachers, Secondary School

- Annual Earnings: $52,900

- Earnings Growth Potential: Low

- Job Growth: 13.3%

- Annual Job Openings: 5,750

- Self-Employed: 0.2%

Teach secondary school subjects to educationally and physically handicapped students. Includes teachers who specialize and work with audibly and visually handicapped students and those who teach basic academic and life processes skills to the mentally impaired. Maintain accurate and complete student records and prepare reports on children and activities as required by laws, district policies, and administrative regulations. Teach socially acceptable behavior, employing techniques such as behavior modification and positive reinforcement. Prepare materials and classrooms for class activities. Establish and enforce rules for behavior and policies and procedures to maintain order among students. Confer with parents, administrators, testing specialists, social workers, and professionals to develop individual educational plans designed to promote students' educational, physical, and social development. Instruct through lectures, discussions, and demonstrations in one or more subjects, such as English, mathematics, or social studies. Employ special educational strategies and techniques during instruction to improve the development of sensory- and perceptual-motor skills, language, cognition, and memory.

Employment Outlook: Employment of these teachers is expected to rise as more students qualify for special education services. Excellent job prospects are expected.

Education of Workforce—Some College: 5.9%. **Associate Degree:** 3.8%. **Bachelor's Degree:** 38.3%. **Master's Degree:** 44.9%. **Doctorate/ Professional Degree:** 2.1%. **Average Age:** 43. **Percentage of Women:** 84.9%.

Skills: Learning Strategies; Social Perceptiveness; Service Orientation; Instructing; Monitoring; Active Learning; Reading Comprehension; Writing. **Personality Type(s):** Social-Investigative. **Work Environment:** Indoors; sounds, noisy; standing.

Tour Guides and Escorts

- Annual Earnings: $23,750

- Earnings Growth Potential: Low

- Job Growth: 11.7%

- Annual Job Openings: 2,060

- Self-Employed: 15.1%

Escort individuals or groups on sightseeing tours or through places of interest such as industrial establishments, public buildings, and art galleries. Conduct educational activities for schoolchildren. Escort individuals or groups on cruises; on sightseeing tours; or through places of interest such as industrial establishments, public buildings, and art galleries. Describe tour points of interest to group members and respond to questions. Monitor visitors' activities to ensure compliance with establishment or tour regulations and safety practices. Greet and register visitors and issue any required identification badges or safety devices. Distribute brochures, show audiovisual presentations, and explain establishment processes and operations at tour sites. Provide directions and other pertinent information to visitors. Provide for physical safety of groups, performing such activities as providing first aid and directing emergency evacuations. Research environmental conditions and clients' skill and ability levels to plan expeditions, instruction, and commentary that are appropriate.

Employment Outlook: About-average employment growth is projected.

Education of Workforce—Some College: 22.8%. **Associate Degree:** 8.6%. **Bachelor's Degree:** 27.5%. **Master's Degree:** 10.8%. **Doctorate/ Professional Degree:** 1.5%. **Average Age:** 44. **Percentage of Women:** No data available.

Skills: Service Orientation; Active Listening; Judgment and Decision Making; Programming; Installation; Operation Monitoring; Operation and Control; Equipment Maintenance. **Personality Type(s):** Social-Enterprising. **Work Environment:** Standing.

Training and Development Managers

- Annual Earnings: $88,090

- Earnings Growth Potential: High

- Job Growth: 11.9%

- Annual Job Openings: 1,010

- Self-Employed: 0.6%

Plan, direct, or coordinate the training and development activities and staff of organizations. Conduct orientation sessions and arrange on-the-job training for new hires. Evaluate instructor performance and the effectiveness of training programs, providing recommendations for improvement. Develop testing and evaluation procedures. Conduct or arrange for ongoing technical training and personal development classes for staff members. Confer with management and conduct surveys to identify training needs based on projected production processes, changes, and other factors. Develop and organize training manuals, multimedia visual aids, and other educational materials. Plan, develop, and provide training and staff development programs, using knowledge of the effectiveness of methods such as classroom training, demonstrations, on-the-job training, meetings, conferences, and workshops. Analyze training needs to develop new training programs or modify and improve existing programs. Review and evaluate training and apprenticeship programs for compliance with government standards.

Employment Outlook: Efforts to recruit and retain employees, the growing importance of employee training, and new legal standards are expected to increase employment of these workers. College graduates and those with certification should have the best opportunities.

Education of Workforce—Some College: 21.7%. **Associate Degree:** 7.4%. **Bachelor's Degree:** 36.3%. **Master's Degree:** 17.8%. **Doctorate/ Professional Degree:** 2.0%. **Average Age:** 45. **Percentage of Women:** No data available.

Skills: Management of Financial Resources; Learning Strategies; Management of Personnel Resources; Instructing; Systems Evaluation; Management of Material Resources; Systems Analysis; Speaking. **Personality Type(s):** Enterprising-Social. **Work Environment:** Indoors; sitting.

Training and Development Specialists

- Annual Earnings: $52,120
- Earnings Growth Potential: High
- Job Growth: 23.3%
- Annual Job Openings: 10,710
- Self-Employed: 1.6%

Conduct training and development programs for employees. Keep up with developments in area of expertise by reading current journals, books, and magazine articles. Present information, using a variety of instructional techniques and formats such as role playing, simulations, team exercises, group discussions, videos, and lectures. Schedule classes based on availability of classrooms, equipment, and instructors. Obtain or organize and develop training procedure manuals and guides and course materials such as handouts and visual materials. Offer specific training programs to help workers maintain or improve job skills. Monitor, evaluate, and record training activities and program effectiveness. Attend meetings and seminars to obtain information for use in training programs or to inform management of training program status. Coordinate recruitment and placement of training program participants. Develop alternative training methods if expected improvements are not seen.

Employment Outlook: Efforts to recruit and retain employees, the growing importance of employee training, and new legal standards are expected to increase employment of these workers. College graduates and those with certification should have the best opportunities.

Education of Workforce—Some College: 22.9%. **Associate Degree:** 9.2%. **Bachelor's Degree:** 37.7%. **Master's Degree:** 13.2%. **Doctorate/ Professional Degree:** 1.8%. **Average Age:** 43. **Percentage of Women:** No data available.

Skills: Operations Analysis; Learning Strategies; Science; Instructing; Systems Evaluation; Writing; Coordination; Social Perceptiveness. **Personality Type(s):** Social-Artistic-Conventional. **Work Environment:** Indoors; sitting.

Tutors

- Annual Earnings: $31,540
- Earnings Growth Potential: High
- Job Growth: 14.7%
- Annual Job Openings: 22,570
- Self-Employed: 20.6%

Job openings are shared with Adaptive Physical Education Specialists and with Teachers and Instructors, All Other.

Provide nonclassroom, academic instruction to students on an individual or small-group basis for proactive or remedial purposes. Travel to students' homes, libraries, or schools to conduct tutoring sessions. Schedule tutoring appointments with students or their parents. Research or recommend textbooks, software, equipment, or other learning materials to complement tutoring. Prepare and facilitate tutoring workshops, collaborative projects, or academic support sessions for small groups of students. Participate in training and development sessions to improve tutoring practices or learn new tutoring techniques. Organize tutoring environment to promote productivity and learning. Monitor student performance or assist students in academic environments, such as classrooms, laboratories, or computing centers. Review class material with students by discussing text, working solutions to problems, or reviewing worksheets or other assignments. Provide feedback to students, using positive reinforcement techniques to encourage, motivate, or build confidence in students.

Employment Outlook: Faster-than-average employment growth is projected.

Education of Workforce—Some College: 19.2%. **Associate Degree:** 8.0%. **Bachelor's Degree:** 35.0%. **Master's Degree:** 20.1%. **Doctorate/ Professional Degree:** 3.4%. **Average Age:** 42. **Percentage of Women:** No data available.

Skills: No data available. **Personality Type(s):** No data available. **Work Environment:** No data available.

Vocational Education Teachers, Middle School

- Annual Earnings: $49,320

- Earnings Growth Potential: Low

- Job Growth: 3.2%

- Annual Job Openings: 410

- Self-Employed: 0.0%

Teach or instruct vocational or occupational subjects at the middle school level. Establish and enforce rules for behavior and procedures for maintaining order among the students for whom they are responsible. Instruct and monitor students in the use and care of equipment and materials to prevent injuries and damage. Instruct students individually and in groups, using various teaching methods such as lectures, discussions, and demonstrations. Maintain accurate and complete student records as required by laws, district policies, and administrative regulations. Prepare materials and classrooms for class activities. Establish clear objectives for all lessons, units, and projects and communicate those objectives to students. Plan and conduct activities for a balanced program of instruction, demonstration, and work time that provides students with opportunities to observe, question, and investigate. Adapt teaching methods and instructional materials to meet students' varying needs and interests.

Employment Outlook: Employment growth for these workers should arise from continued increases in school enrollments, but growth will be limited by the focus on traditional academic subjects. Prospects are expected to be favorable as workers leave the occupation permanently.

Education of Workforce—Some College: 2.9%. **Associate Degree:** 2.1%. **Bachelor's Degree:** 46.5%. **Master's Degree:** 44.4%. **Doctorate/ Professional Degree:** 2.9%. **Average Age:** 43. **Percentage of Women:** 81.2%.

Skills: Learning Strategies; Operations Analysis; Instructing; Social Perceptiveness; Systems Evaluation; Management of Personnel Resources; Speaking; Writing. **Personality Type(s):** Social-Artistic-Conventional. **Work Environment:** Indoors; standing; sounds, noisy; using your hands to handle, control, or feel objects, tools, or controls.

Vocational Education Teachers, Postsecondary

- Annual Earnings: $47,950
- Earnings Growth Potential: High
- Job Growth: 15.1%
- Annual Job Openings: Roughly 4,000
- Self-Employed: 0.2%

Job openings are an estimated portion of those shared with 37 other postsecondary teaching occupations.

Teach or instruct vocational or occupational subjects at the postsecondary level (but at less than the baccalaureate) to students who have graduated or left high school. Includes correspondence school instructors; industrial, commercial, and government training instructors; and adult education teachers and instructors who prepare persons to operate industrial machinery and equipment and transportation and communications equipment. Teaching may take place in public or private schools whose primary business is education or in a school associated with an organization whose primary business is other than education. Supervise and monitor students' use of tools and equipment. Observe and evaluate students' work to determine progress, provide feedback, and make suggestions for improvement. Present lectures and conduct discussions to increase students' knowledge and competence, using visual aids such as graphs, charts, videotapes, and slides. Administer oral, written, or performance tests to measure progress and to evaluate training effectiveness. Prepare reports and maintain records such as student grades, attendance rolls, and training activity details. Supervise independent or group projects, field placements, laboratory work, or other training. Determine training needs of students or workers. Provide individualized instruction and tutorial or remedial instruction. Conduct on-the-job training, classes, or training sessions to teach and demonstrate principles, techniques, procedures, and methods of designated subjects. Develop curricula and plan course content and methods of instruction.

Employment Outlook: Enrollments in postsecondary institutions are expected to continue rising as more people attend college and as workers return to school to update their skills. Opportunities for part-time or temporary positions should be favorable, but significant competition exists for tenure-track positions.

Education of Workforce—Some College: 2.7%. **Associate Degree:** 2.3%. **Bachelor's Degree:** 15.3%. **Master's Degree:** 34.6%. **Doctorate/ Professional Degree:** 44.2%. **Average Age:** 45. **Percentage of Women:** No data available.

Skills: Instructing; Learning Strategies; Writing; Operations Analysis; Speaking; Active Learning; Monitoring; Reading Comprehension. **Personality Type(s):** Social-Realistic. **Work Environment:** Indoors; standing; using your hands to handle, control, or feel objects, tools, or controls.

Vocational Education Teachers, Secondary School

- Annual Earnings: $52,550
- Earnings Growth Potential: Low
- Job Growth: 9.6%
- Annual Job Openings: 3,850
- Self-Employed: 0.0%

Teach or instruct vocational or occupational subjects at the secondary school level. Prepare materials and classroom for class activities. Maintain accurate and complete student records as required by law, district policy, and administrative regulations. Instruct students individually and in groups, using various teaching methods, such as lectures, discussions, and demonstrations. Establish and enforce rules for behavior and procedures for maintaining order among students. Observe and evaluate students' performance, behavior, social development, and physical health. Instruct and monitor students in the use and care of equipment and materials to prevent injury and damage. Plan and conduct activities for a balanced program of instruction, demonstration, and work time that provides students with opportunities to observe, question, and investigate. Prepare, administer, and grade tests and assignments to evaluate students' progress. Enforce all administration policies and rules governing students. Assign and grade classwork and homework.

Employment Outlook: Employment growth for these workers should arise from continued increases in school enrollments, but growth will be limited by the focus on traditional academic subjects. Prospects are expected to be favorable as workers leave the occupation permanently.

Education of Workforce—Some College: 2.3%. **Associate Degree:** 1.6%. **Bachelor's Degree:** 45.3%. **Master's Degree:** 46.5%. **Doctorate/ Professional Degree:** 3.3%. **Average Age:** 43. **Percentage of Women:** 56.0%.

Skills: Learning Strategies; Instructing; Persuasion; Negotiation; Systems Evaluation; Social Perceptiveness; Coordination; Mathematics. **Personality Type(s):** Social. **Work Environment:** Indoors; standing; sounds, noisy; using your hands to handle, control, or feel objects, tools, or controls; contaminants; walking and running.

CHAPTER 4

The Advocacy Sequel

Is there something you feel strongly about? Maybe you care passionately about global warming, hunger, human rights, animal rights, property rights, a deadly disease, historic preservation, or some other important issue. Instead of just getting worked up about it, maybe you could *do* something about it. Your chances for making a difference are particularly good if you are well informed about the issue through work experience or have work-related skills that can help advance your pet cause. Have you thought about parlaying that work experience into a career in which you advocate for your favorite cause?

What Advocates Do

One way people create change is by changing the laws. In our political system, legislators do this. Legislators usually have a thorough understanding of the existing laws, at least in one area of expertise. (They have legislative staff and lobbyists to inform them about other areas.) Because politics is the art of the possible, legislators generally construct new laws in ways that will build a consensus among their fellow legislators and the voting public. Often they work out the details in committee meetings and hearings that enable these stakeholders and others to offer their suggestions and buy into the proposed legislation.

Of course, politicians must answer to the opinions of voters. Similarly, businesses must answer to the preferences of consumers. Many professionals work in public relations to shape the attitudes that drive voting and purchasing behaviors. Public relations workers may create campaigns that advocate for change in the law, in government policy, and in corporate actions. Campaigns can be aimed at many kinds of behaviors—think of Smokey the Bear. Public relations workers may raise funds for research, a candidate's political advertising, a university, or a public facility such as a museum or monument. They may work as lobbyists, communicating their talking points directly to legislators.

Another way to achieve change is through existing laws. You can work to compel the enforcement of laws that are being neglected or are being enforced too narrowly. Or you can compel a person, company, or even a government agency to change its behavior by suing for damages. Our democracy allows any citizen to petition an agency or file a legal brief, but lawyers are the workers who make a career out of this kind of action. They are assisted by paralegals and law clerks.

Yet one more way to work for change is through the media. Journalists and news analysts often arouse public interest in political, social, cultural, and business issues. Recently, some bloggers have become as influential as workers in the more traditional media. Speechwriters also communicate opinions. Although someone else serves as the writer's mouthpiece and usually has considerable control over the content, you can choose to work for someone whose outlook you share.

In the table at the end of Chapter 1, you saw the most prominent skills that O*NET lists for advocacy occupations. Now, also from O*NET, here are the most important **work activities** that you would do as an advocate:

- Communicating with people outside the organization, representing the organization to customers, the public, government, and other external sources. This information can be exchanged in person, in writing, or by telephone or e-mail.

- Developing specific goals and plans to prioritize, organize, and accomplish your work.

- Developing constructive and cooperative working relationships with others and maintaining them over time.

- Observing, receiving, and otherwise obtaining information from all relevant sources.

- Providing information to supervisors, co-workers, and subordinates by telephone, in written form, by e-mail, or in person.

- Keeping up to date technically and applying new knowledge to your job.

- Analyzing information and evaluating results to choose the best solution and solve problems.

- Handling complaints, settling disputes, and resolving grievances and conflicts or otherwise negotiating with others.

- Identifying the underlying principles, reasons, or facts of information by breaking down information or data into separate parts.

- Compiling, coding, categorizing, calculating, tabulating, auditing, or verifying information or data.

The Pros and Cons of Advocacy

The average earnings for the 10 advocacy occupations included in this chapter is $65,760, compared to an average of $39,374 for all nonadvocacy occupations. But this average is not very meaningful because the earnings vary so greatly among the various jobs included. Even *within* a single occupation, Lawyers, earnings vary enormously. Lawyers working in beverage and tobacco product manufacturing (some of whom are defending these manufacturers from lawsuits and hostile legislation) earn an average of $193,770 per year, whereas those working in religious, grantmaking, civic, professional, and similar organizations average $113,980.

The BLS projects 17.2% growth for the advocacy occupations from 2008 to 2018 and an average of 7,278 job openings per year.

The O*NET database reports these **work environment** characteristics for the advocacy occupations:

- Indoors, Environmentally Controlled

- Importance of Being Exact or Accurate

- Structured versus Unstructured Work

- Time Pressure

- Frequency of Decision Making

- Freedom to Make Decisions

- Impact of Decisions on Co-workers or Company Results

- Spend Time Sitting

- Frequency of Conflict Situations

- Deal with Unpleasant or Angry People

Advocates work under some pressure, but they make many independent decisions. Not all of their efforts succeed in advancing the causes they care about, and sometimes they confront people who disagree strongly. Nevertheless, they enjoy the rewards of at least trying to make a difference.

How to Move into Advocacy

People who are elected to political office come from many backgrounds. For example, Representative Tom DeLay of Texas earned a bachelor's degree in biology, worked for a pesticide manufacturer, and then started a highly successful extermination business. When the Environmental Protection Agency banned a pesticide that was in wide use, DeLay decided to advocate for reducing government regulation of businesses. He volunteered as a Republican precinct chairman and eventually ran for a seat in the Texas legislature, which was his springboard to Congress.

President Barack Obama entered politics after working as a lawyer and law professor, but he was greatly influenced by his earlier work as a community organizer. That experience educated him about the needs of working people and how politics operates at the grassroots level.

Politics and other advocacy careers offer many opportunities for gaining experience through volunteer work. Find a local organization that works for the cause that motivates you and offer your services. If no such organization exists, start one. Advocacy groups need all kinds of volunteer workers, but if you're interested in a career in advocacy, you should play a role that gives you appropriate experience. For example, you could write position papers and press releases, research legal issues, speak at public meetings, arrange meetings with legislators, manage a fund drive, or canvass voters. Chapter 10 offers a script you can follow to volunteer for an advocacy organization.

For suggestions about moving into a sequel career in the media, see Chapter 6.

Descriptions of Advocacy Occupations

The O*NET database includes 10 jobs related to advocacy. Some advocacy-related job titles that you may be familiar with are considered specializations within these titles. For Lobbyist, see Public Relations Specialists; for Fund Raiser, see Public Relations Managers; for Community Advocate, see Social and Human Service Assistants; and for Community Organizer, see Social Workers, All Other.

Broadcast News Analysts

- Annual Earnings: $50,400

- Earnings Growth Potential: High

- Job Growth: 4.2%

- Annual Job Openings: 240

- Self-Employed: 19.3%

Analyze, interpret, and broadcast news received from various sources.
Analyze and interpret news and information received from various sources
in order to be able to broadcast the information. Write commentar-
ies, columns, or scripts, using computers. Examine news items of local,
national, and international significance to determine topics to address or
obtain assignments from editorial staff members. Coordinate and serve
as an anchor on news broadcast programs. Edit news material to ensure
that it fits within available time or space. Select material most pertinent to
presentation and organize this material into appropriate formats. Gather
information and develop perspectives about news subjects through research,
interviews, observation, and experience. Present news stories and introduce
in-depth videotaped segments or live transmissions from on-the-scene
reporters.

Employment Outlook: Consolidation in publishing and broadcasting is
expected to result in job losses for these workers. Competition is expected
to be keen at major newspapers and stations; smaller newspapers and stations should provide better opportunities.

Education of Workforce—Some College: 9.8%. **Associate Degree:**
3.6%. **Bachelor's Degree:** 59.8%. **Master's Degree:** 21.1%. **Doctorate/
Professional Degree:** 2.3%. **Average Age:** 41. **Percentage of Women:**
45.4%.

Skills: Speaking; Writing; Social Perceptiveness; Reading Comprehension;
Critical Thinking; Active Listening; Persuasion; Active Learning.
Personality Type(s): Artistic-Social-Enterprising. **Work Environment:**
Indoors; sitting; making repetitive motions; sounds, noisy.

Law Clerks

- Annual Earnings: $38,390
- Earnings Growth Potential: High
- Job Growth: 13.9%
- Annual Job Openings: 1,080
- Self-Employed: 14.0%

Assist lawyers or judges by researching or preparing legal documents. May meet with clients or assist lawyers and judges in court. Search for and study legal documents to investigate facts and law of cases, to determine causes of action, and to prepare cases. Prepare affidavits of documents and maintain document files and case correspondence. Review and file pleadings, petitions, and other documents relevant to court actions.

Employment Outlook: Faster-than-average employment growth is projected.

Education of Workforce—Some College: 27.4%. **Associate Degree:** 13.5%. **Bachelor's Degree:** 27.0%. **Master's Degree:** 6.6%. **Doctorate/ Professional Degree:** 4.3%. **Average Age:** 42. **Percentage of Women:** 74.5%.

Skills: Critical Thinking; Reading Comprehension; Writing; Active Listening; Active Learning; Speaking; Persuasion; Negotiation. **Personality Type(s):** Conventional-Investigative-Enterprising. **Work Environment:** Indoors; sitting; making repetitive motions.

Lawyers

- Annual Earnings: $113,240
- Earnings Growth Potential: Very high
- Job Growth: 13.0%
- Annual Job Openings: 24,040
- Self-Employed: 26.2%

Represent clients in criminal and civil litigation and other legal proceedings, draw up legal documents, and manage or advise clients on legal transactions. May specialize in a single area or may practice broadly in many areas of law. Represent clients in court or before government agencies. Select jurors, argue motions, meet with judges, and question witnesses during the course of a trial. Present evidence to defend clients or prosecute defendants in criminal or civil litigation. Interpret laws, rulings, and regulations for individuals and businesses. Study Constitution, statutes, decisions, regulations, and ordinances of quasi-judicial bodies to determine ramifications for cases. Present and summarize cases to judges and juries. Prepare legal briefs and opinions and file appeals in state and federal courts of appeal. Analyze the probable outcomes of cases, using knowledge of legal precedents. Examine legal data to determine advisability of defending or prosecuting lawsuits. Evaluate findings and develop strategies and arguments in preparation for presentation of cases. Advise clients concerning business transactions, claim liability, advisability of prosecuting or defending lawsuits, or legal rights and obligations.

Employment Outlook: Growth in both population and business activity is expected to result in more civil disputes and criminal cases and, thus, employment growth for lawyers. This growth is expected to be constrained, however, as paralegals and other workers perform some of the tasks previously done by lawyers. Keen competition is expected.

Education of Workforce—Some College: 0.8%. **Associate Degree:** 0.3%. **Bachelor's Degree:** 2.5%. **Master's Degree:** 3.0%. **Doctorate/ Professional Degree:** 92.8%. **Average Age:** 46. **Percentage of Women:** 34.5%.

Skills: Persuasion; Negotiation; Speaking; Writing; Critical Thinking; Judgment and Decision Making; Active Learning; Active Listening. **Personality Type(s):** Enterprising-Investigative. **Work Environment:** Indoors; sitting.

Legislators

- Annual Earnings: $18,810

- Earnings Growth Potential: Very low

- Job Growth: 0.7%

- Annual Job Openings: 1,970

- Self-Employed: 0.0%

Develop laws and statutes at the federal, state, or local level. Attend receptions, dinners, and conferences to meet people, exchange views and information, and develop working relationships. Analyze and understand the local and national implications of proposed legislation. Represent their government at local, national, and international meetings and conferences. Promote the industries and products of their electoral districts. Oversee expense allowances, ensuring that accounts are balanced at the end of each fiscal year. Organize and maintain campaign organizations and fundraisers in order to raise money for election or re-election. Evaluate the structure, efficiency, activities, and performance of government agencies. Establish personal offices in local districts or states and manage office staff. Encourage and support party candidates for political office. Conduct "head counts" to help predict the outcome of upcoming votes. Speak to students to encourage and support the development of future political leaders.

Employment Outlook: Little or no employment growth is projected.

Education of Workforce—Some College: 16.9%. **Associate Degree:** 5.7%. **Bachelor's Degree:** 38.6%. **Master's Degree:** 19.0%. **Doctorate/ Professional Degree:** 6.2%. **Average Age:** No data available. **Percentage of Women:** No data available.

Skills: No data available. **Personality Type(s):** Enterprising-Social. **Work Environment:** No data available.

Paralegals and Legal Assistants

- Annual Earnings: $46,980

- Earnings Growth Potential: Medium

- Job Growth: 28.1%

- Annual Job Openings: 10,400

- Self-Employed: 3.2%

Assist lawyers by researching legal precedent, investigating facts, or preparing legal documents. Conduct research to support a legal proceeding, to formulate a defense, or to initiate legal action. Prepare affidavits or other documents, such as legal correspondence, and organize and maintain documents in paper or electronic filing system. Prepare for trial by performing tasks such as organizing exhibits. Prepare legal documents, including briefs, pleadings, appeals, wills, contracts, and real estate closing statements. Meet with clients and other professionals to discuss details of case. File pleadings with court clerk. Gather and analyze research data, such as statutes; decisions; and legal articles, codes, and documents. Call upon witnesses to testify at hearings. Investigate facts and law of cases and search pertinent sources, such as public records, to determine causes of action and to prepare cases. Direct and coordinate law office activity, including delivery of subpoenas. Keep and monitor legal volumes to ensure that law library is up to date. Appraise and inventory real and personal property for estate planning.

Employment Outlook: Increased demand for accessible, cost-efficient legal services is expected to increase employment for paralegals, who may perform more tasks previously done by lawyers. Keen competition is expected. Experienced, formally trained paralegals should have the best job prospects.

Education of Workforce—Some College: 26.6%. **Associate Degree:** 18.4%. **Bachelor's Degree:** 33.7%. **Master's Degree:** 4.1%. **Doctorate/ Professional Degree:** 2.4%. **Average Age:** 43. **Percentage of Women:** 74.5%.

Skills: Writing; Active Listening; Speaking; Quality Control Analysis; Operation and Control; Equipment Maintenance; Troubleshooting; Repairing. **Personality Type(s):** Conventional-Investigative-Enterprising. **Work Environment:** Indoors; sitting; making repetitive motions.

Public Relations Managers

- Annual Earnings: $89,690

- Earnings Growth Potential: High

- Job Growth: 12.9%

- Annual Job Openings: 2,060

- Self-Employed: 0.0%

Plan and direct public relations programs designed to create and maintain a favorable public image for employer or client or, if engaged in fundraising, plan and direct activities to solicit and maintain funds for special projects and nonprofit organizations. Establish and maintain effective working relationships with clients, government officials, and media representatives and use these relationships to develop new business opportunities. Write interesting and effective press releases, prepare information for media kits, and develop and maintain company Internet or intranet Web pages. Identify main client groups and audiences, determine the best way to communicate publicity information to them, and develop and implement a communication plan. Assign, supervise, and review the activities of public relations staff. Develop and maintain the company's corporate image and identity, which includes the use of logos and signage. Respond to requests for information about employers' activities or status. Direct activities of external agencies, establishments, and departments that develop and implement communication strategies and information programs. Manage communications budgets.

Employment Outlook: Job growth is expected to result from companies' need to distinguish their products and services in an increasingly competitive marketplace. Keen competition is expected.

Education of Workforce—Some College: 14.1%. **Associate Degree:** 5.9%. **Bachelor's Degree:** 46.5%. **Master's Degree:** 20.9%. **Doctorate/ Professional Degree:** 2.7%. **Average Age:** 45. **Percentage of Women:** 60.3%.

Skills: Management of Financial Resources; Persuasion; Management of Material Resources; Negotiation; Management of Personnel Resources; Systems Evaluation; Systems Analysis; Coordination. **Personality Type(s):** Enterprising-Artistic. **Work Environment:** Indoors; sitting.

Public Relations Specialists

- Annual Earnings: $51,960

- Earnings Growth Potential: High

- Job Growth: 24.0%

- Annual Job Openings: 13,130

- Self-Employed: 4.5%

Engage in promoting or creating goodwill for individuals, groups, or organizations by writing or selecting favorable publicity material and releasing it through various communications media. May prepare and arrange displays and make speeches. Respond to requests for information from the media or designate another appropriate spokesperson or information source. Study the objectives, promotional policies, and needs of organizations to develop public relations strategies that will influence public opinion or promote ideas, products, and services. Plan and direct development and communication of informational programs to maintain favorable public and stockholder perceptions of an organization's accomplishments and agenda. Establish and maintain cooperative relationships with representatives of community, consumer, employee, and public interest groups.

Prepare or edit organizational publications for internal and external audiences, including employee newsletters and stockholders' reports. Coach client representatives in effective communication with the public and with employees. Confer with production and support personnel to produce or coordinate production of advertisements and promotions.

Employment Outlook: As the business environment becomes increasingly globalized, the need for good public relations and communications is growing rapidly. Opportunities should be best for workers with knowledge of more than one language.

Education of Workforce—Some College: 11.9%. **Associate Degree:** 4.0%. **Bachelor's Degree:** 55.3%. **Master's Degree:** 18.3%. **Doctorate/ Professional Degree:** 3.2%. **Average Age:** 40. **Percentage of Women:** 61.6%.

Skills: Operations Analysis; Social Perceptiveness; Negotiation; Writing; Systems Evaluation; Speaking; Persuasion; Time Management. **Personality Type(s):** Enterprising-Artistic-Social. **Work Environment:** Indoors; sitting.

Reporters and Correspondents

- Annual Earnings: $34,360

- Earnings Growth Potential: High

- Job Growth: –7.6%

- Annual Job Openings: 1,690

- Self-Employed: 19.3%

Collect and analyze facts about newsworthy events by interview, investigation, or observation. Report and write stories for newspaper, news magazine, radio, or television. Report and write news stories for publication or broadcast, describing the background and details of events. Arrange interviews with people who can provide information about a particular story. Review copy and correct errors in content, grammar, and punctuation, following prescribed editorial style and formatting guidelines. Review and evaluate notes taken about event aspects to isolate pertinent facts and details. Determine a story's emphasis, length, and format and organize material accordingly. Research and analyze background information related to stories in order to be able to provide complete and accurate information. Gather information about events through research; interviews; experience;

and attendance at political, news, sports, artistic, social, and other functions. Investigate breaking news developments such as disasters, crimes, and human interest stories.

Employment Outlook: Consolidation in publishing and broadcasting is expected to result in job losses for these workers. Competition is expected to be keen at major newspapers and stations; smaller newspapers and stations should provide better opportunities.

Education of Workforce—Some College: 9.8%. **Associate Degree:** 3.6%. **Bachelor's Degree:** 59.8%. **Master's Degree:** 21.1%. **Doctorate/ Professional Degree:** 2.3%. **Average Age:** 41. **Percentage of Women:** 45.4%.

Skills: Writing; Speaking; Active Listening; Critical Thinking; Reading Comprehension; Social Perceptiveness; Judgment and Decision Making; Complex Problem Solving. **Personality Type(s):** Artistic-Enterprising-Investigative. **Work Environment:** More often indoors than outdoors; sounds, noisy; sitting.

Social and Human Service Assistants

- Annual Earnings: $27,940

- Earnings Growth Potential: Low

- Job Growth: 22.6%

- Annual Job Openings: 15,390

- Self-Employed: 0.3%

Assist professionals from a wide variety of fields such as psychology, rehabilitation, or social work to provide client services, as well as support for families. May assist clients in identifying available benefits and social and community services and help clients obtain them. May assist social workers with developing, organizing, and conducting programs to prevent and resolve problems relevant to substance abuse, human relationships, rehabilitation, or adult day care. Keep records and prepare reports for owner or management concerning visits with clients. Submit reports and review reports or problems with superiors. Interview individuals and family members to compile information on social, educational, criminal, institutional, or drug histories. Provide information and refer individuals to public or private agencies or community services for assistance. Consult with supervisors concerning programs for individual families. Advise clients regarding food stamps, child care, food, money management, sanitation, or housekeeping. Oversee day-to-day group activities of residents in institution. Visit individuals in homes or attend group meetings to provide information on agency services, requirements, and procedures. Monitor free, supplementary meal program to ensure cleanliness of facility and that eligibility guidelines are met for persons receiving meals. Meet with youth groups to acquaint them with consequences of delinquent acts.

Employment Outlook: As the elderly population grows, demand for the services provided by these workers is expected to increase. Opportunities are expected to be excellent, particularly for job seekers with some postsecondary education, such as a certificate or associate degree in a related subject.

Education of Workforce—Some College: 20.9%. **Associate Degree:** 9.6%. **Bachelor's Degree:** 37.1%. **Master's Degree:** 13.4%. **Doctorate/ Professional Degree:** 1.3%. **Average Age:** 42. **Percentage of Women:** No data available.

Skills: Social Perceptiveness; Service Orientation; Active Listening; Science; Systems Analysis; Speaking; Learning Strategies; Persuasion. **Personality Type(s):** Conventional-Social-Enterprising. **Work Environment:** Indoors; sitting.

Social Workers, All Other

- Annual Earnings: $49,420

- Earnings Growth Potential: High

- Job Growth: 12.8%

- Annual Job Openings: 2,780

- Self-Employed: 2.2%

All social workers not listed separately. No task data available.

Employment Outlook: The rapidly increasing elderly population is expected to spur demand for social services. Job prospects should be favorable because of the need to replace the many workers who are leaving the occupation permanently.

Education of Workforce—Some College: 10.4%. **Associate Degree:** 6.0%. **Bachelor's Degree:** 42.3%. **Master's Degree:** 32.2%. **Doctorate/Professional Degree:** 1.6%. **Average Age:** 43. **Percentage of Women:** 79.4%.

Skills: No data available. **Personality Type(s):** No data available. **Work Environment:** No data available.

CHAPTER 5

The Standards-Enforcement Sequel

From your experience on your previous job, you understand the difference between good work and hack work in your field. Perhaps you know harmful results that substandard business practices or products can produce. This knowledge can be the basis of your next job.

What Standards Enforcers Do

Some standards enforcers are essentially cops. They protect the public from illegal acts and harmful products such as hiring discrimination, air pollution, buildings that are firetraps, tainted food products, toxic paint on toys, and defective seatbelts. They conduct inspections, review records, perform tests, and take measurements that indicate compliance with the law or a violation. Like cops, they need to know the fine points of the laws that they are enforcing and the procedures for correcting or punishing those who violate those laws.

Some of these enforcers stay in one setting throughout the workday. For example, some equal opportunity representatives work in the human resources office of a large business and review the company's hiring and promotion practices by checking records and interviewing staff. Other enforcement workers must travel between sites where they conduct inspections. Environmental compliance inspectors may take air or water samples at various locations; agricultural inspectors may visit several farms or food-processing plants in a workday.

Not all standards enforcers are responsible for upholding the law; some help a business to ensure the quality of its products or services. They make certain that your food will not make you sick, that your car will run properly, and that your pants will not split the first time you wear them.

Management does not want to disappoint consumers, especially because news about schlock merchandise can spread quickly. So quality control workers sample the output and measure it against industry standards. When they find defects, they determine the cause. And they do more than just prevent substandard output. The current trend in management is to accomplish constant improvement of quality. So quality control workers find ways to exceed industry standards.

In the table at the end of Chapter 1, you saw the most prominent skills that O*NET lists for the standards-enforcement occupations. Now, also from O*NET, here are the most important **work activities** that you would do to enforce standards:

- Keeping up to date technically and applying new knowledge to your job.

- Developing constructive and cooperative working relationships with others and maintaining them over time.

- Communicating with people outside the organization, representing the organization to customers, the public, government, and other external sources. This information can be exchanged in person, in writing, or by telephone or e-mail.

- Using relevant information and individual judgment to determine whether events or processes comply with laws, regulations, or standards.

- Providing information to supervisors, co-workers, and subordinates by telephone, in written form, by e-mail, or in person.

- Observing, receiving, and otherwise obtaining information from all relevant sources.

- Identifying information by categorizing, estimating, recognizing differences or similarities, and detecting changes in circumstances or events.

- Compiling, coding, categorizing, calculating, tabulating, auditing, or verifying information or data.

- Analyzing information and evaluating results to choose the best solution and solve problems.

- Developing specific goals and plans to prioritize, organize, and accomplish your work.

The Pros and Cons of Standards Enforcement

The 18 standards-enforcement occupations included in this chapter are linked to 13 occupations surveyed by the Bureau of Labor Statistics. They have average earnings of $62,148, compared to an average of $39,320 for all other occupations.

The BLS projects 16.4% growth for the standards-enforcement occupations from 2008 to 2018 and an average of 6,564 job openings per year.

The O*NET database reports these **work environment** characteristics for the standards-enforcement occupations:

- Importance of Being Exact or Accurate
- Freedom to Make Decisions
- Indoors, Environmentally Controlled
- Impact of Decisions on Co-workers or Company Results
- Frequency of Decision Making
- Structured versus Unstructured Work
- Time Pressure
- Frequency of Conflict Situations
- Deal with Unpleasant or Angry People
- Spend Time Sitting

Maybe you've heard the joke about the guy whose job it is to sort potatoes into bags of small, medium, and large spuds. His complaint about the job: "Decisions, decisions!" What makes the joke funny is that the decisions the man must make, though unending, are really of very little consequence; great fortunes are not riding on his ability to make extremely precise judgments about potato size. In real-life jobs, however, enforcing standards can sometimes have a very large impact. The impact can be beneficial, even life-saving. But it can also create conflict with the company or person whose output you judge as substandard. That's one reason the decision-making aspect of the job can be stressful. Also, standards enforcers need to make their decisions within a structure of rules and procedures that sometimes can feel arbitrary and confining.

How to Move into Standards Enforcement

In addition to relevant work experience, some law-enforcement jobs in this field require certification or licensure. Usually you must pass an exam that demonstrates your knowledge of the laws. You will face this requirement especially for jobs that relate to safety, such as Construction and Building Inspectors. For some jobs, however, such as Occupational Health and Safety Specialists, licensing is uncommon and certification is voluntary. For these jobs, an appropriate education and work experience are more important.

People work in quality control at all levels, from the low-skilled potato sorters (who can easily be replaced by machines) to quality control systems managers and industrial engineers, who are highly skilled with using statistical techniques to create product-sampling schedules and make sense of the data derived from them. These workers generally have at least a bachelor's degree. Several organizations and universities offer graduate-level training that prepares you to pass a certification exam in quality control. Various kinds of science and engineering technicians, often with two-year degrees, support these workers.

There are formal and informal ways to move into standards enforcement. Think about who maintains the quality of output in your current job. Or consider who ensures the safety of your workplace or protects the environment in your community. Ask these people how they got their job and whether your experience in your work role would be a helpful background to do this work.

If you're aware of some aspect of quality control or safety that's being neglected where you work (or at a similar workplace), maybe you can create a new job for yourself. Prepare a business plan for a program, with you in charge, that will address this need. Be sure to include estimates of the costs and, if possible, the payback to the company from increased sales or the smaller risk of a lawsuit. Then propose this plan to management. If you're not knowledgeable enough to design and manage a quality control program, maybe you can convince management to bring in an appropriately qualified professional whom you can support as a technician.

Descriptions of Standards-Enforcement Occupations

It's possible to specialize in quality control in almost any occupation, but this chapter features job descriptions of 18 occupations from the O*NET database that are related to standards enforcement.

Agricultural Inspectors

- Annual Earnings: $41,500
- Earnings Growth Potential: Medium
- Job Growth: 12.8%
- Annual Job Openings: 550
- Self-Employed: 0.0%

Inspect agricultural commodities, processing equipment, and facilities and fish and logging operations to ensure compliance with regulations and laws governing health, quality, and safety. Set standards for the production of meat and poultry products and for food ingredients, additives, and compounds used to prepare and package products. Direct and monitor the quarantine and treatment or destruction of plants and plant products. Monitor the operations and sanitary conditions of slaughtering and meat processing plants. Verify that transportation and handling procedures meet regulatory requirements. Take emergency actions such as closing production facilities if product safety is compromised. Set labeling standards and approve labels for meat and poultry products. Review and monitor foreign product inspection systems in countries of origin to ensure equivalence to the U.S. system. Inspect the cleanliness and practices of establishment employees. Advise farmers and growers of development programs or new equipment and techniques to aid in quality production. Inspect livestock to determine effectiveness of medication and feeding programs.

Employment Outlook: Federal and state governments, the largest employers of these workers, are not expected to hire a significant number of new inspectors. Job prospects should be good to replace the many agricultural inspectors expected to leave the occupation permanently.

Education of Workforce—Some College: 25.0%. **Associate Degree:**
8.1%. **Bachelor's Degree:** 24.1%. **Master's Degree:** 4.2%. **Doctorate/
Professional Degree:** 1.4%. **Average Age:** 49. **Percentage of Women:**
18.5%.

Skills: Quality Control Analysis; Science; Operation Monitoring;
Monitoring; Systems Evaluation; Systems Analysis; Speaking;
Troubleshooting. **Personality Type(s):** Realistic-Conventional-
Investigative. **Work Environment:** More often indoors than outdoors;
contaminants; very hot or cold temperatures; sounds, noisy; standing.

Aviation Inspectors

- Annual Earnings: $56,290

- Earnings Growth Potential: High

- Job Growth: 18.4%

- Annual Job Openings: 1,130

- Self-Employed: 4.2%

*Job openings are shared with Freight and Cargo Inspectors and with Transportation
Vehicle, Equipment and Systems Inspectors, Except Aviation.*

**Inspect aircraft, maintenance procedures, air navigational aids, air traf-
fic controls, and communications equipment to ensure conformance
with federal safety regulations.** Inspect work of aircraft mechanics performing maintenance, modification, or repair and overhaul of aircraft and
aircraft mechanical systems to ensure adherence to standards and procedures. Start aircraft and observe gauges, meters, and other instruments to
detect evidence of malfunctions. Examine aircraft access plates and doors
for security. Examine landing gear, tires, and exteriors of fuselage, wings,
and engines for evidence of damage or corrosion and to determine whether
repairs are needed. Prepare and maintain detailed repair, inspection, investigation, and certification records and reports. Inspect new, repaired, or
modified aircraft to identify damage or defects and to assess airworthiness
and conformance to standards, using checklists, hand tools, and test instruments. Examine maintenance records and flight logs to determine if
service and maintenance checks and overhauls were performed at prescribed
intervals.

Employment Outlook: Faster-than-average employment growth is projected.

Education of Workforce—Some College: 32.2%. **Associate Degree:** 12.5%. **Bachelor's Degree:** 12.0%. **Master's Degree:** 2.3%. **Doctorate/ Professional Degree:** 0.1%. **Average Age:** 49. **Percentage of Women:** 11.3%.

Skills: Science; Equipment Maintenance; Troubleshooting; Repairing; Operation and Control; Equipment Selection; Quality Control Analysis; Operation Monitoring. **Personality Type(s):** Realistic-Conventional-Investigative. **Work Environment:** More often indoors than outdoors; sounds, noisy; sitting.

Construction and Building Inspectors

- Annual Earnings: $51,530

- Earnings Growth Potential: Medium

- Job Growth: 16.8%

- Annual Job Openings: 3,970

- Self-Employed: 7.5%

Inspect structures, using engineering skills to determine structural soundness and compliance with specifications, building codes, and other regulations. Inspections may be general in nature or may be limited to a specific area, such as electrical systems or plumbing. Issue violation notices and stop-work orders, conferring with owners, violators, and authorities to explain regulations and recommend rectifications. Inspect bridges, dams, highways, buildings, wiring, plumbing, electrical circuits, sewers, heating systems, and foundations during and after construction for structural quality, general safety, and conformance to specifications and codes. Approve and sign plans that meet required specifications. Review and interpret plans, blueprints, site layouts, specifications, and construction methods to ensure compliance to legal requirements and safety regulations. Monitor installation of plumbing, wiring, equipment, and appliances to ensure that installation is performed properly and is in compliance with applicable regulations. Inspect and monitor construction sites to ensure adherence to safety standards, building codes, and specifications.

Employment Outlook: Employment growth is expected to be driven by desires for safety and improved quality of construction. Prospects should be best for workers who have some college education, certification, and construction experience.

Education of Workforce—Some College: 32.7%. **Associate Degree:** 12.8%. **Bachelor's Degree:** 21.4%. **Master's Degree:** 2.7%. **Doctorate/ Professional Degree:** 0.4%. **Average Age:** 50. **Percentage of Women:** 9.5%.

Skills: Science; Quality Control Analysis; Operation and Control; Systems Evaluation; Mathematics; Systems Analysis; Operation Monitoring; Persuasion. **Personality Type(s):** Realistic-Conventional-Investigative. **Work Environment:** More often outdoors than indoors; very hot or cold temperatures; contaminants; extremely bright or inadequate lighting; cramped work space, awkward positions.

Environmental Compliance Inspectors

- Annual Earnings: $49,750

- Earnings Growth Potential: Medium

- Job Growth: 31.0%

- Annual Job Openings: 10,850

- Self-Employed: 1.4%

Job openings are shared with Coroners; Equal Opportunity Representatives and Officers; Government Property Inspectors and Investigators; Licensing Examiners and Inspectors; and Regulatory Affairs Specialists.

Inspect and investigate sources of pollution to protect the public and environment and ensure conformance with federal, state, and local regulations and ordinances. Determine the nature of code violations and actions to be taken and issue written notices of violation; participate in enforcement hearings as necessary. Examine permits, licenses, applications, and records to ensure compliance with licensing requirements. Prepare, organize, and maintain inspection records. Interview individuals to determine the nature of suspected violations and to obtain evidence of violations. Prepare written, oral, tabular, and graphic reports summarizing requirements and regulations, including enforcement and chain of custody documentation. Monitor follow-up actions in cases where violations were found and review compliance monitoring reports. Investigate complaints and suspected violations regarding illegal dumping, pollution, pesticides, product quality, or labeling laws. Inspect waste pretreatment, treatment, and disposal facilities and systems for conformance to federal, state, or local regulations.

Employment Outlook: Much-faster-than-average employment growth is projected.

Education of Workforce—Some College: 20.9%. **Associate Degree:** 10.3%. **Bachelor's Degree:** 36.9%. **Master's Degree:** 14.1%. **Doctorate/ Professional Degree:** 3.8%. **Average Age:** 45. **Percentage of Women:** No data available.

Skills: Quality Control Analysis; Science; Troubleshooting; Mathematics; Reading Comprehension; Writing; Systems Evaluation; Active Learning. **Personality Type(s):** Conventional-Investigative-Realistic. **Work Environment:** More often indoors than outdoors; sitting; contaminants.

Equal Opportunity Representatives and Officers

- Annual Earnings: $49,750

- Earnings Growth Potential: Medium

- Job Growth: 31.0%

- Annual Job Openings: 10,850

- Self-Employed: 1.4%

Job openings are shared with Coroners; Environmental Compliance Inspectors; Government Property Inspectors and Investigators; Licensing Examiners and Inspectors; and Regulatory Affairs Specialists.

Monitor and evaluate compliance with equal opportunity laws, guidelines, and policies to ensure that employment practices and contracting arrangements give equal opportunity without regard to race, religion, color, national origin, sex, age, or disability. Investigate employment practices and alleged violations of laws in order to document and correct discriminatory factors. Interpret civil rights laws and equal opportunity regulations for individuals and employers. Study equal opportunity complaints in order to clarify issues. Meet with persons involved in equal opportunity complaints in order to verify case information and to arbitrate and settle disputes. Coordinate, monitor, and revise complaint procedures to ensure timely processing and review of complaints. Prepare reports of selection, survey, and other statistics and recommendations for corrective action. Conduct surveys and evaluate findings in order to determine if systematic discrimination exists. Develop guidelines for nondiscriminatory employment practices and monitor their implementation and impact. Review company contracts to determine actions required to meet governmental equal opportunity provisions.

Employment Outlook: Much-faster-than-average employment growth is projected.

Education of Workforce—Some College: 20.9%. **Associate Degree:** 10.3%. **Bachelor's Degree:** 36.9%. **Master's Degree:** 14.1%. **Doctorate/ Professional Degree:** 3.8%. **Average Age:** 45. **Percentage of Women:** No data available.

Skills: Persuasion; Reading Comprehension; Active Listening; Active Learning; Negotiation; Writing; Systems Evaluation; Speaking. **Personality Type(s):** Social-Enterprising-Conventional. **Work Environment:** Indoors; sitting; making repetitive motions.

First-Line Supervisors/Managers of Production and Operating Workers

- Annual Earnings: $52,060

- Earnings Growth Potential: Medium

- Job Growth: –5.2%

- Annual Job Openings: 9,190

- Self-Employed: 4.6%

Supervise and coordinate the activities of production and operating workers, such as inspectors, precision workers, machine setters and operators, assemblers, fabricators, and plant and system operators. Enforce safety and sanitation regulations. Direct and coordinate the activities of employees engaged in the production or processing of goods, such as inspectors, machine setters, and fabricators. Read and analyze charts, work orders, production schedules, and other records and reports to determine production requirements and to evaluate current production estimates and outputs. Confer with other supervisors to coordinate operations and activities within or between departments. Plan and establish work schedules, assignments, and production sequences to meet production goals. Inspect materials, products, or equipment to detect defects or malfunctions. Demonstrate equipment operations and work and safety procedures to new employees or assign employees to experienced workers for training. Observe work and monitor gauges, dials, and other indicators to ensure that operators conform to production or processing standards.

Employment Outlook: Slow decline in employment is projected.

Education of Workforce—Some College: 25.2%. **Associate Degree:** 7.7%. **Bachelor's Degree:** 11.8%. **Master's Degree:** 2.7%. **Doctorate/ Professional Degree:** 0.4%. **Average Age:** No data available. **Percentage of Women:** 18.1%.

Skills: Management of Personnel Resources; Management of Material Resources; Operations Analysis; Negotiation; Systems Analysis; Coordination; Time Management; Quality Control Analysis. **Personality Type(s):** Enterprising-Realistic-Conventional. **Work Environment:** Indoors; sounds, noisy; standing; contaminants; walking and running; hazardous equipment.

Food Scientists and Technologists

- Annual Earnings: $59,630
- Earnings Growth Potential: High
- Job Growth: 16.3%
- Annual Job Openings: 690
- Self-Employed: 12.5%

Use chemistry, microbiology, engineering, and other sciences to study the principles underlying the processing and deterioration of foods; analyze food content to determine levels of vitamins, fat, sugar, and protein; discover new food sources; research ways to make processed foods safe, palatable, and healthful; and apply food science knowledge to determine the best ways to process, package, preserve, store, and

distribute food. Test new products for flavor, texture, color, nutritional content, and adherence to government and industry standards. Check raw ingredients for maturity or stability for processing and finished products for safety, quality, and nutritional value. Confer with process engineers, plant operators, flavor experts, and packaging and marketing specialists to resolve problems in product development. Evaluate food processing and storage operations and assist in the development of quality assurance programs for such operations. Study methods to improve aspects of foods, such as chemical composition, flavor, color, texture, nutritional value, and convenience. Study the structure and composition of food or the changes foods undergo in storage and processing. Develop new or improved ways of preserving, processing, packaging, storing, and delivering foods, using knowledge of chemistry, microbiology, and other sciences.

Employment Outlook: Job growth is expected to stem primarily from efforts to increase the quantity and quality of food for a growing population and to balance output with protection and preservation of soil, water, and ecosystems. Opportunities should be good for agricultural and food scientists in almost all fields.

Education of Workforce—Some College: 8.9%. **Associate Degree:** 7.5%. **Bachelor's Degree:** 41.4%. **Master's Degree:** 23.4%. **Doctorate/ Professional Degree:** 14.2%. **Average Age:** 43. **Percentage of Women:** No data available.

Skills: Science; Quality Control Analysis; Systems Evaluation; Systems Analysis; Negotiation; Complex Problem Solving; Writing; Active Learning. **Personality Type(s):** Investigative-Realistic-Conventional. **Work Environment:** Indoors; sitting; sounds, noisy.

Fraud Examiners, Investigators, and Analysts

- Annual Earnings: $58,350

- Earnings Growth Potential: Medium

- Job Growth: 10.5%

- Annual Job Openings: 4,320

- Self-Employed: 0.9%

Job openings are shared with Financial Quantitative Analysts; Investment Underwriters; and Risk Management Specialists.

Obtain evidence, take statements, produce reports, and testify to findings regarding resolution of fraud allegations. May coordinate fraud detection and prevention activities. Maintain knowledge of current events and trends in such areas as money laundering and criminal tools and techniques. Train others in fraud detection and prevention techniques. Research or evaluate new technologies for use in fraud detection systems. Prepare evidence for presentation in court. Negotiate with responsible parties to arrange for recovery of losses due to fraud. Conduct field surveillance to gather case-related information. Testify in court regarding investigation findings. Advise businesses or agencies on ways to improve fraud detection. Review reports of suspected fraud to determine need for further investigation. Prepare written reports of investigation findings. Recommend actions in fraud cases. Lead or participate in fraud investigation teams. Interview witnesses or suspects and take statements. Design, implement, or maintain fraud detection tools or procedures. Gather financial documents related to investigations.

Employment Outlook: About-average employment growth is projected.

Education of Workforce—Some College: 21.1%. **Associate Degree:** 10.0%. **Bachelor's Degree:** 34.1%. **Master's Degree:** 13.9%. **Doctorate/Professional Degree:** 2.9%. **Average Age:** 42. **Percentage of Women:** 57.0%.

Skills: Writing; Negotiation; Active Listening; Speaking; Reading Comprehension; Systems Evaluation; Systems Analysis; Persuasion. **Personality Type(s):** Enterprising-Investigative-Conventional. **Work Environment:** Indoors; sitting.

Freight and Cargo Inspectors

- Annual Earnings: $56,290

- Earnings Growth Potential: High

- Job Growth: 18.4%

- Annual Job Openings: 1,130

- Self-Employed: 4.2%

Job openings are shared with Aviation Inspectors and with Transportation Vehicle, Equipment and Systems Inspectors, Except Aviation.

Inspect the handling, storage, and stowing of freight and cargoes.
Prepare and submit reports after completion of freight shipments. Inspect shipments to ensure that freight is securely braced and blocked. Record details about freight conditions, handling of freight, and any problems encountered. Advise crews in techniques of stowing dangerous and heavy cargo. Observe loading of freight to ensure that crews comply with procedures. Recommend remedial procedures to correct any violations found during inspections. Inspect loaded cargo, cargo lashed to decks or in storage facilities, and cargo-handling devices to determine compliance with health and safety regulations and need for maintenance. Measure ships' holds and depths of fuel and water in tanks, using sounding lines and tape measures. Notify workers of any special treatment required for shipments. Direct crews to reload freight or to insert additional bracing or packing as necessary.

Employment Outlook: Faster-than-average employment growth is projected.

Education of Workforce—Some College: 32.2%. **Associate Degree:** 12.5%. **Bachelor's Degree:** 12.0%. **Master's Degree:** 2.3%. **Doctorate/Professional Degree:** 0.1%. **Average Age:** 49. **Percentage of Women:** 11.3%.

Skills: Operation and Control; Quality Control Analysis; Operation Monitoring; Management of Personnel Resources; Writing; Troubleshooting; Equipment Maintenance; Installation. **Personality Type(s):** Realistic-Conventional. **Work Environment:** More often outdoors than indoors; sounds, noisy; contaminants; very hot or cold temperatures; extremely bright or inadequate lighting.

Government Property Inspectors and Investigators

- Annual Earnings: $49,750
- Earnings Growth Potential: Medium
- Job Growth: 31.0%
- Annual Job Openings: 10,850
- Self-Employed: 1.4%

Job openings are shared with Coroners; Environmental Compliance Inspectors; Equal Opportunity Representatives and Officers; Licensing Examiners and Inspectors; and Regulatory Affairs Specialists.

Investigate or inspect government property to ensure compliance with contract agreements and government regulations. Prepare correspondence, reports of inspections or investigations, and recommendations for action. Inspect government-owned equipment and materials in the possession of private contractors to ensure compliance with contracts and regulations and to prevent misuse. Examine records, reports, and documents to establish facts and detect discrepancies. Inspect manufactured or processed products to ensure compliance with contract specifications and legal requirements. Locate and interview plaintiffs, witnesses, or representatives of business or government to gather facts relevant to inspections or alleged violations. Recommend legal or administrative action to protect government property. Submit samples of products to government laboratories for testing as required. Coordinate with and assist law enforcement agencies in matters of mutual concern. Testify in court or at administrative proceedings concerning findings of investigations. Collect, identify, evaluate, and preserve case evidence.

Employment Outlook: Much-faster-than-average employment growth is projected.

Education of Workforce—Some College: 20.9%. **Associate Degree:** 10.3%. **Bachelor's Degree:** 36.9%. **Master's Degree:** 14.1%. **Doctorate/ Professional Degree:** 3.8%. **Average Age:** 45. **Percentage of Women:** No data available.

Skills: Quality Control Analysis; Persuasion; Systems Evaluation; Writing; Operation and Control; Speaking; Judgment and Decision Making; Operation Monitoring. **Personality Type(s):** Conventional-Enterprising-Realistic. **Work Environment:** More often outdoors than indoors; sounds, noisy; contaminants; very hot or cold temperatures; sitting.

Industrial Engineering Technicians

- Annual Earnings: $46,760
- Earnings Growth Potential: Low
- Job Growth: 6.6%
- Annual Job Openings: 1,850
- Self-Employed: 0.7%

Apply engineering theory and principles to problems of industrial layout or manufacturing production, usually under the direction of engineering staff. May study and record time, motion, method, and speed involved in performance of production, maintenance, clerical, and other worker operations for such purposes as establishing standard production rates or improving efficiency. Recommend revision to methods of operation, material handling, equipment layout, or other changes to increase production or improve standards. Study time, motion, methods, and speed involved in maintenance, production, and other operations to establish standard production rate and improve efficiency. Interpret engineering drawings, schematic diagrams, or formulas and confer with management or engineering staff to determine quality and reliability standards. Recommend modifications to existing quality or production standards to achieve optimum quality within limits of equipment capability. Aid in planning work assignments in accordance with worker performance, machine capacity, production schedules, and anticipated delays. Observe workers using equipment to verify that equipment is being operated and maintained according to quality assurance standards. Observe workers operating equipment or performing tasks to determine time involved and fatigue rate, using timing devices.

Employment Outlook: Labor-saving efficiencies and the automation of many engineering support activities will limit the need for new engineering technicians. In general, opportunities should be best for job seekers who have an associate degree or other postsecondary training in engineering technology.

Education of Workforce—Some College: 33.1%. **Associate Degree:** 22.7%. **Bachelor's Degree:** 14.1%. **Master's Degree:** 2.3%. **Doctorate/ Professional Degree:** 0.5%. **Average Age:** 44. **Percentage of Women:** No data available.

Skills: Technology Design; Mathematics; Systems Evaluation; Monitoring; Systems Analysis; Quality Control Analysis; Judgment and Decision Making; Active Learning. **Personality Type(s):** Investigative-Realistic-Conventional. **Work Environment:** Indoors; contaminants; sounds, noisy; standing; hazardous equipment; walking and running.

Industrial Engineers

- Annual Earnings: $75,110
- Earnings Growth Potential: Low
- Job Growth: 14.2%
- Annual Job Openings: 8,540
- Self-Employed: 0.7%

Job openings are shared with Human Factors Engineers and Ergonomists.

Design, develop, test, and evaluate integrated systems for managing industrial production processes, including human work factors, quality control, inventory control, logistics and material flow, cost analysis, and production coordination. Develop manufacturing methods, labor utilization standards, and cost analysis systems to promote efficient staff and facility utilization. Recommend methods for improving utilization of personnel, material, and utilities. Plan and establish sequence of operations to fabricate and assemble parts or products and to promote efficient utilization. Apply statistical methods and perform mathematical calculations to determine manufacturing processes, staff requirements, and production standards. Draft and design layout of equipment, materials, and workspace to illustrate maximum efficiency, using drafting tools and computer. Review production schedules, engineering specifications, orders, and related information to obtain knowledge of manufacturing methods, procedures, and activities. Communicate with management and user personnel to develop production and design standards.

Employment Outlook: Competitive pressures and advancing technology are expected to result in businesses hiring more engineers. Overall, job opportunities are expected to be good. Professional, scientific, and technical services industries should generate most of the employment growth.

Education of Workforce—Some College: 13.5%. **Associate Degree:** 10.2%. **Bachelor's Degree:** 49.2%. **Master's Degree:** 16.6%. **Doctorate/Professional Degree:** 2.1%. **Average Age:** 44. **Percentage of Women:** 14.9%.

Skills: Management of Material Resources; Management of Financial Resources; Mathematics; Systems Evaluation; Systems Analysis; Reading Comprehension; Complex Problem Solving; Writing. **Personality Type(s):** Investigative-Conventional-Enterprising. **Work Environment:** Indoors; sounds, noisy; contaminants; sitting; hazardous equipment.

Licensing Examiners and Inspectors

- Annual Earnings: $49,750

- Earnings Growth Potential: Medium

- Job Growth: 31.0%

- Annual Job Openings: 10,850

- Self-Employed: 1.4%

Job openings are shared with Coroners; Environmental Compliance Inspectors; Equal Opportunity Representatives and Officers; Government Property Inspectors and Investigators; and Regulatory Affairs Specialists.

Examine, evaluate, and investigate eligibility for, conformity with, or liability under licenses or permits. Issue licenses to individuals meeting standards. Evaluate applications, records, and documents in order to gather information about eligibility or liability issues. Administer oral, written, road, or flight tests to license applicants. Score tests and observe equipment operation and control in order to rate ability of applicants. Advise licensees and other individuals or groups concerning licensing, permit, or passport regulations. Warn violators of infractions or penalties. Prepare reports of activities, evaluations, recommendations, and decisions. Prepare correspondence to inform concerned parties of licensing decisions and of appeals processes. Confer with and interview officials, technical or professional specialists, and applicants in order to obtain information or to clarify facts relevant to licensing decisions. Report law or regulation violations to appropriate boards and agencies.

Employment Outlook: Much-faster-than-average employment growth is projected.

Education of Workforce—Some College: 20.9%. **Associate Degree:** 10.3%. **Bachelor's Degree:** 36.9%. **Master's Degree:** 14.1%. **Doctorate/ Professional Degree:** 3.8%. **Average Age:** 45. **Percentage of Women:** No data available.

Skills: Quality Control Analysis; Judgment and Decision Making; Social Perceptiveness; Speaking; Operation Monitoring; Service Orientation; Systems Evaluation; Reading Comprehension. **Personality Type(s):** Conventional-Enterprising. **Work Environment:** More often indoors than outdoors; making repetitive motions; contaminants; using your hands to handle, control, or feel objects, tools, or controls; sitting.

Management Analysts

- Annual Earnings: $75,250

- Earnings Growth Potential: High

- Job Growth: 23.9%

- Annual Job Openings: 30,650

- Self-Employed: 25.8%

Conduct organizational studies and evaluations, design systems and procedures, conduct work simplifications and measurement studies, and prepare operations and procedures manuals to assist management in operating more efficiently and effectively. Includes program analysts and management consultants. Gather and organize information on problems or procedures. Analyze data gathered and develop solutions or alternative methods of proceeding. Confer with personnel concerned to ensure successful functioning of newly implemented systems or procedures. Develop and implement records management program for filing, protection, and retrieval of records and assure compliance with program. Review forms and reports and confer with management and users about format, distribution, and purpose and to identify problems and improvements. Document findings of study and prepare recommendations for implementation of new systems, procedures, or organizational changes. Interview personnel and conduct on-site observation to ascertain unit functions; work performed; and methods, equipment, and personnel used. Prepare manuals and train workers in use of new forms, reports, procedures, or equipment according to organizational policy. Design, evaluate, recommend, and approve changes of forms and reports.

Employment Outlook: Organizations are expected to rely increasingly on outside expertise in an effort to maintain competitiveness and improve performance. Keen competition is expected. Opportunities are expected to be best for those who have a graduate degree, specialized expertise, and ability in salesmanship and public relations.

Education of Workforce—Some College: 12.5%. **Associate Degree:** 5.0%. **Bachelor's Degree:** 40.4%. **Master's Degree:** 28.8%. **Doctorate/Professional Degree:** 6.8%. **Average Age:** 47. **Percentage of Women:** 43.5%.

Skills: Operations Analysis; Systems Evaluation; Systems Analysis; Judgment and Decision Making; Writing; Management of Personnel Resources; Instructing; Persuasion. **Personality Type(s):** Investigative-Enterprising-Conventional. **Work Environment:** Indoors; sitting.

Occupational Health and Safety Specialists

- Annual Earnings: $63,230
- Earnings Growth Potential: Medium
- Job Growth: 11.2%
- Annual Job Openings: 2,490
- Self-Employed: 0.7%

Review, evaluate, and analyze work environments and design programs and procedures to control, eliminate, and prevent diseases or injuries caused by chemical, physical, and biological agents or ergonomic factors. Order suspension of activities that pose threats to workers' health and safety. Recommend measures to help protect workers from potentially hazardous work methods, processes, or materials. Investigate accidents to identify causes and to determine how such accidents might be prevented in the future. Investigate the adequacy of ventilation, exhaust equipment, lighting, and other conditions that could affect employee health, comfort, or performance. Develop and maintain hygiene programs such as noise surveys, continuous atmosphere monitoring, ventilation surveys, and asbestos management plans. Inspect and evaluate workplace environments, equipment, and practices in order to ensure compliance with safety standards and government regulations. Collaborate with engineers and physicians to institute control and remedial measures for hazardous and potentially hazardous conditions or equipment. Conduct safety training and education programs and demonstrate the use of safety equipment.

Employment Outlook: These workers will be needed to ensure workplace safety in response to changing hazards, regulations, public expectations, and technology.

Education of Workforce—Some College: 16.7%. **Associate Degree:** 8.4%. **Bachelor's Degree:** 39.1%. **Master's Degree:** 20.7%. **Doctorate/ Professional Degree:** 2.1%. **Average Age:** 44. **Percentage of Women:** No data available.

Skills: Science; Operations Analysis; Quality Control Analysis; Operation Monitoring; Persuasion; Troubleshooting; Systems Evaluation; Systems Analysis. **Personality Type(s):** Investigative-Conventional. **Work Environment:** More often indoors than outdoors; sounds, noisy; sitting; contaminants.

Quality Control Analysts

- Annual Earnings: $42,110
- Earnings Growth Potential: High
- Job Growth: 13.3%
- Annual Job Openings: 3,640
- Self-Employed: 1.6%

Job openings are shared with Precision Agriculture Technicians and Remote Sensing Technicians.

Conduct tests to determine quality of raw materials, bulk intermediate, and finished products. May conduct stability sample tests. Train other analysts to perform laboratory procedures and assays. Perform visual inspections of finished products. Serve as a technical liaison between quality control and other departments, vendors, or contractors. Participate in internal assessments and audits as required. Identify and troubleshoot equipment

The Sequel: How to Change Your Career Without Starting Over

problems. Evaluate new technologies and methods to make recommendations regarding their use. Ensure that lab cleanliness and safety standards are maintained. Develop and qualify new testing methods. Coordinate testing with contract laboratories and vendors. Write technical reports or documentation such as deviation reports, testing protocols, and trend analyses. Write or revise standard quality control operating procedures. Supply quality control data necessary for regulatory submissions. Receive and inspect raw materials. Review data from contract laboratories to ensure accuracy and regulatory compliance.

Employment Outlook: About-average employment growth is projected.

Education of Workforce—Some College: 23.9%. **Associate Degree:** 12.6%. **Bachelor's Degree:** 29.7%. **Master's Degree:** 9.4%. **Doctorate/ Professional Degree:** 4.2%. **Average Age:** 37. **Percentage of Women:** No data available.

Skills: No data available. **Personality Type(s):** Conventional-Investigative-Realistic. **Work Environment:** No data available.

Quality Control Systems Managers

- Annual Earnings: $85,080

- Earnings Growth Potential: Medium

- Job Growth: –7.7%

- Annual Job Openings: 5,470

- Self-Employed: 1.3%

Job openings are shared with Biofuels Production Managers; Biomass Production Managers; Geothermal Production Managers; Hydroelectric Production Managers; and Methane/Landfill Gas Collection System Operators.

Plan, direct, or coordinate quality assurance programs. Formulate quality control policies and control quality of laboratory and production efforts. Stop production if serious product defects are present. Review and approve quality plans submitted by contractors. Review statistical studies, technological advances, or regulatory standards and trends to stay abreast of issues in the field of quality control. Generate and maintain quality control operating budgets. Evaluate new testing and sampling methodologies or technologies to determine usefulness. Coordinate the selection and implementation of quality control equipment such as inspection gauges. Collect and analyze production samples to evaluate quality. Audit and inspect subcontractor facilities, including external laboratories. Verify that raw materials, purchased parts or components, in-process samples, and finished products meet established testing and inspection standards. Review quality documentation necessary for regulatory submissions and inspections. Review and update standard operating procedures or quality assurance manuals.

Employment Outlook: Increased domestic labor productivity and rising imports are expected to reduce the need for these managers. Job seekers who have experience in production occupations—along with a degree in industrial engineering, management, or business administration—should have the best job prospects.

Education of Workforce—Some College: 23.2%. **Associate Degree:** 9.2%. **Bachelor's Degree:** 30.2%. **Master's Degree:** 10.7%. **Doctorate/ Professional Degree:** 1.2%. **Average Age:** 46. **Percentage of Women:** 14.5%.

Skills: No data available. **Personality Type(s):** Enterprising-Conventional-Realistic. **Work Environment:** No data available.

Transportation Vehicle, Equipment, and Systems Inspectors, Except Aviation

- Annual Earnings: $56,290

- Earnings Growth Potential: High

- Job Growth: 18.4%

- Annual Job Openings: 1,130

- Self-Employed: 4.2%

Job openings are shared with Aviation Inspectors and with Freight and Cargo Inspectors.

Inspect and monitor transportation equipment, vehicles, or systems to ensure compliance with regulations and safety standards. Conduct vehicle or transportation equipment tests, using diagnostic equipment. Investigate and make recommendations on carrier requests for waiver of federal standards. Prepare reports on investigations or inspections and actions taken. Issue notices and recommend corrective actions when infractions or problems are found. Investigate incidents or violations such as delays, accidents, and equipment failures. Investigate complaints regarding safety violations. Inspect repairs to transportation vehicles and equipment to ensure that repair work was performed properly. Examine transportation vehicles, equipment, or systems to detect damage, wear, or malfunction. Inspect vehicles and other equipment for evidence of abuse, damage, or mechanical malfunction. Examine carrier operating rules, employee qualification guidelines, and carrier training and testing programs for compliance with regulations or safety standards.

Employment Outlook: Faster-than-average employment growth is projected.

Education of Workforce—Some College: 32.2%. **Associate Degree:** 12.5%. **Bachelor's Degree:** 12.0%. **Master's Degree:** 2.3%. **Doctorate/ Professional Degree:** 0.1%. **Average Age:** 49. **Percentage of Women:** 11.3%.

Skills: Equipment Maintenance; Repairing; Troubleshooting; Science; Operation and Control; Quality Control Analysis; Operation Monitoring; Equipment Selection. **Personality Type(s):** Realistic-Conventional-Investigative. **Work Environment:** Contaminants; using your hands to handle, control, or feel objects, tools, or controls; sounds, noisy; very hot or cold temperatures; cramped work space, awkward positions; hazardous equipment.

CHAPTER 6

The Communications Sequel

One way to use your trove of workplace knowledge is to communicate it to other people who want or need to know it. This kind of sequel career overlaps somewhat with two other sequels. If you're communicating to help people master new skills, you're engaged primarily in teaching, which is covered by Chapter 3. Or if you're communicating to express a point of view, the job may fall in the category of advocacy, which is described in Chapter 4.

This chapter focuses on using your knowledge to *inform* people. The jobs covered here are in what the Department of Labor calls the information industry, but that term sometimes gets misunderstood when people assume it means information technology—that is, computers. These jobs are about communicating knowledge, not processing data. Also, they focus on the content of what's being communicated rather than the technology being used for communication.

What Communicators Do

Like teachers, communicators transfer knowledge to increase people's understanding. Often the job involves explaining unfamiliar concepts or making inferences from facts. Communicators have to avoid boring or confusing their knowledge-consumers. To do this, they must be careful to organize their accumulated knowledge in ways that will be meaningful to readers and listeners. For example, they use logical structures, build a general case by using specific examples, or call attention to contrasts and similarities. They also must find effective wording and, in today's media, often supporting graphic or sound content. A few of them speak on television or radio and need the appropriate skills for engaging their viewers and listeners.

Some of them work in news media as journalists, analysts, or editors. Recently, online news media have begun to rival print, radio, and television for the attention of the public. Other communicators write or edit nonfiction articles, books, and Web pages, often on how-to and lifestyle subjects such as home repair, personal financial management, cooking, health and fitness, travel, the arts, or (as in the book you're now reading) career development. Some work as critics, communicating their opinions of books, movies, plays, musical performances, wines, restaurants, or other subjects that are matters of taste, where expert judgment is respected.

Interpreters and translators communicate across language differences. Knowledge of a technical subject can be very useful in some settings—for example, to translate a technical manual or do medical interpreting.

Compared to these other communicators, technical writers are less concerned with avoiding boredom and more concerned with avoiding confusion and misunderstanding. They transfer technical knowledge, usually for use in the workplace, although sometimes about complex consumer products.

Copy writers prepare advertising copy and other promotional materials. Their task is a mixture of informing and persuading.

Some communicators compile data that people will find useful. You're already familiar with the large businesses that compile phone numbers, stock quotations, and sports scores. Some small companies, known as information brokers, compile business directories offering more localized or specific information than Hoovers, Dun & Bradstreet, or the Yellow Pages can provide.

In the table at the end of Chapter 1, you saw the most prominent skills that O*NET lists for the communications occupations. Now, also from O*NET, here are the most important **work activities** that you would do as a communicator:

- Communicating with people outside the organization, representing the organization to customers, the public, government, and other external sources. This information can be exchanged in person, in writing, or by telephone or e-mail.

- Developing specific goals and plans to prioritize, organize, and accomplish your work.

- Keeping up to date technically and applying new knowledge to your job.

- Developing constructive and cooperative working relationships with others and maintaining them over time.

- Developing, designing, or creating new applications, ideas, relationships, systems, or products, including artistic contributions.

- Providing information to supervisors, co-workers, and subordinates by telephone, in written form, by e-mail, or in person.

- Observing, receiving, and otherwise obtaining information from all relevant sources.

- Identifying information by categorizing, estimating, recognizing differences or similarities, and detecting changes in circumstances or events.

- Scheduling events, programs, and activities, as well as the work of others.

- Analyzing information and evaluating results to choose the best solution and solve problems.

The Pros and Cons of Communications

The average earnings for the eight communications jobs surveyed by the BLS are $50,440, compared to an average of $39,668 for all other occupations.

The BLS projects 14.5% growth for the communications occupations from 2008 to 2018 and an average of 4,724 job openings per year.

The O*NET database reports these **work environment** characteristics for communicators:

- Indoors, Environmentally Controlled

- Spend Time Sitting

- Importance of Being Exact or Accurate

- Structured versus Unstructured Work

- Time Pressure

- Freedom to Make Decisions

- Impact of Decisions on Co-workers or Company Results

- Frequency of Decision Making

- Level of Competition

- Spend Time Making Repetitive Motions

People like their information even fresher than the food they eat, so communicators work under pressure to turn out content quickly. Information consumers also prize accuracy and learn to avoid careless or biased communicators, except in subjects (such as politics or advertising) where slanted content is expected or even preferred. Communicators have to compete for the attention of a public that is bombarded by media during almost every waking hour. However, the work allows considerable independent thinking and provides the satisfaction of enlightening the public, sometimes making their lives easier or persuading them to a point of view. Although some aspects of the work are structured and often involve long hours at the computer keyboard, it also provides considerable opportunities for creativity.

How to Move into Communications

Every job involves some communications: e-mails, memos, letters, reports, phone conversations. If you are interested in these tasks, you can ask for assignments that give you opportunities to practice and improve your communications skills. For example, ask to write the first draft of the report for a project you're involved in. You may be able to do this as a Web page, slide presentation, or even a video. A portfolio of these documents can help you get a job that focuses primarily on this communication role.

Another highly useful way to get experience and add to your portfolio is in a volunteer organization. Find a social, political, religious, sporting, business, or community group that you feel comfortable with. Perhaps best of all would be an organization that has use for knowledge you acquired in your work. Offer to write for the organization's newsletter, weekly e-mails, press releases, annual report, Web page, or other media outlet. Or write speeches for the organization's leaders.

Certification is generally required for medical and legal interpreters. The training program, offered at some colleges, usually includes supervised work experience.

The Web offers many low-cost opportunities to reach a large audience. For example, a blog can get national exposure for your writing. In fact, some blogs are paying, full-time jobs for their writers. Some bloggers interview industry leaders and publish the interviews, either as text or as podcasts.

You might also start a small information-brokering business—for example, compiling a directory with detailed and timely information on businesses and important people in your industry. This gives you a legitimate reason to phone or e-mail many people in your industry on a regular basis.

One advantage of being a hub of industry information, whether through blogging, podcasting, or information brokering, is that your information-gathering and dissemination efforts will enlarge your network of contacts in the industry. Even if your blog or information business fails to turn a profit, it will boost your visibility and your awareness of news, so it may lead to job opportunities in some other work function.

If your industry is in decline, you may have increasing difficulty finding readers or listeners for your messages. But once you have developed a port-folio that demonstrates your communications skills, you can shift your focus to subjects that are in greater demand. In other words, this sequel career can serve as your bridge from a shrinking industry to an expanding one.

Descriptions of Communications Occupations

The O*NET database includes eight occupations that work in communications in a nontechnical capacity.

Broadcast News Analysts

For job description, see Chapter 4.

Copy Writers

- Annual Earnings: $53,900
- Earnings Growth Potential: High
- Job Growth: 14.8%
- Annual Job Openings: 5,420
- Self-Employed: 69.4%

Job openings are shared with Poets, Lyricists, and Creative Writers.

Write advertising copy for use by publication or broadcast media to promote sale of goods and services. Write to customers in their terms and on their level so that the advertiser's sales message is more readily received. Discuss the product, advertising themes and methods, and any changes that should be made in advertising copy with the client. Write advertising copy for use by publication, broadcast, or Internet media to promote the sale of goods and services. Present drafts and ideas to clients. Vary language and tone of messages based on product and medium. Consult with sales, media, and marketing representatives to obtain information on product or service and discuss style and length of advertising copy. Edit or rewrite existing copy as necessary and submit copy for approval by supervisor. Develop advertising campaigns for a wide range of clients, working with an advertising agency's creative director and art director to determine the best way to present advertising information.

Employment Outlook: Projected job growth for these workers stems from increased use of online media and growing demand for Web-based information. But print publishing is expected to continue weakening. Job competition should be keen.

Education of Workforce—Some College: 9.6%. **Associate Degree:** 3.2%. **Bachelor's Degree:** 47.9%. **Master's Degree:** 26.2%. **Doctorate/ Professional Degree:** 9.0%. **Average Age:** 47. **Percentage of Women:** 57.3%.

Skills: Writing; Persuasion; Reading Comprehension; Negotiation; Active Listening; Management of Personnel Resources; Speaking; Critical Thinking. **Personality Type(s):** Enterprising-Artistic. **Work Environment:** Indoors; sitting.

Editors

- Annual Earnings: $50,800
- Earnings Growth Potential: High
- Job Growth: –0.3%
- Annual Job Openings: 3,390
- Self-Employed: 12.1%

Perform variety of editorial duties, such as laying out, indexing, and revising content of written materials, in preparation for final publication. Prepare, rewrite, and edit copy to improve readability or supervise others who do this work. Verify facts, dates, and statistics, using standard reference sources. Read copy or proof to detect and correct errors in spelling, punctuation, and syntax. Develop story or content ideas, considering reader or audience appeal. Review and approve proofs submitted by composing room prior to publication production. Supervise and coordinate work of reporters and other editors. Plan the contents of publications according to the publication's style, editorial policy, and publishing requirements. Read, evaluate, and edit manuscripts or other materials submitted for publication and confer with authors regarding changes in content, style or organization, or publication. Allocate print space for story text, photos, and illustrations according to space parameters and copy significance, using knowledge of layout principles.

Employment Outlook: Projected job growth for these workers stems from increased use of online media and growing demand for Web-based information. But print publishing is expected to continue weakening. Job competition should be keen.

Education of Workforce—Some College: 10.9%. **Associate Degree:** 4.0%. **Bachelor's Degree:** 55.6%. **Master's Degree:** 20.3%. **Doctorate/ Professional Degree:** 4.6%. **Average Age:** 43. **Percentage of Women:** 54.8%.

Skills: Writing; Reading Comprehension; Quality Control Analysis; Negotiation; Management of Personnel Resources; Time Management; Persuasion; Active Learning. **Personality Type(s):** Artistic-Enterprising-Conventional. **Work Environment:** Indoors; sitting; making repetitive motions; using your hands to handle, control, or feel objects, tools, or controls; sounds, noisy.

Interpreters and Translators

- Annual Earnings: $40,860

- Earnings Growth Potential: High

- Job Growth: 22.2%

- Annual Job Openings: 2,340

- Self-Employed: 26.1%

Translate or interpret written, oral, or sign language text into another language for others. Follow ethical codes that protect the confidentiality of information. Identify and resolve conflicts related to the meanings of words, concepts, practices, or behaviors. Proofread, edit, and revise translated materials. Translate messages simultaneously or consecutively into specified languages orally or by using hand signs, maintaining message content, context, and style as much as possible. Check translations of technical terms and terminology to ensure that they are accurate and remain consistent throughout translation revisions. Read written materials such as legal documents, scientific works, or news reports and rewrite material into specified languages. Refer to reference materials such as dictionaries, lexicons, encyclopedias, and computerized terminology banks as needed to ensure translation accuracy. Compile terminology and information to be used in translations, including technical terms such as those for legal or medical material. Adapt translations to students' cognitive and grade levels, collaborating with educational team members as necessary. Listen to speakers' statements to determine meanings and to prepare translations, using electronic listening systems as necessary. Check original texts or confer with authors to ensure that translations retain the content, meaning, and feeling of the original material. Compile information about the content and context of information to be translated, as well as details of the groups for whom translation or interpretation is being performed. Discuss translation requirements with clients and determine any fees to be charged for services provided. Adapt software and accompanying technical documents to another language and culture. Educate students, parents, staff, and teachers about the roles and functions of educational interpreters. Train and supervise other translators/interpreters. Travel with or guide tourists who speak another language.

Employment Outlook: Globalization and large increases in the number of nonnative English speakers in the United States are expected to lead to employment increases for these workers. Job prospects vary by specialty and language.

Education of Workforce—Some College: 23.6%. **Associate Degree:** 14.2%. **Bachelor's Degree:** 30.2%. **Master's Degree:** 13.9%. **Doctorate/ Professional Degree:** 4.4%. **Average Age:** 43. **Percentage of Women:** No data available.

Skills: Writing; Reading Comprehension; Active Listening; Speaking; Social Perceptiveness; Service Orientation; Learning Strategies; Monitoring. **Personality Type(s):** Artistic-Social. **Work Environment:** Indoors; sitting; making repetitive motions.

Poets, Lyricists, and Creative Writers

- Annual Earnings: $53,900

- Earnings Growth Potential: High

- Job Growth: 14.8%

- Annual Job Openings: 5,420

- Self-Employed: 69.4%

Job openings are shared with Copy Writers.

Create original written works, such as scripts, essays, prose, poetry, or song lyrics, for publication or performance. Revise written material to meet personal standards and to satisfy needs of clients, publishers, directors, or producers. Choose subject matter and suitable form to express personal feelings and experiences or ideas or to narrate stories or events. Plan project arrangements or outlines and organize material accordingly. Prepare works in appropriate format for publication and send them to publishers or producers. Follow appropriate procedures to get copyrights for completed work. Write fiction or nonfiction prose such as short stories, novels, biographies, articles, descriptive or critical analyses, and essays. Develop factors such as themes, plots, characterizations, psychological analyses, historical environments, action, and dialogue to create material. Confer with clients, editors, publishers, or producers to discuss changes or revisions to written material. Conduct research to obtain factual information and authentic detail, using sources such as newspaper accounts, diaries, and interviews. Write narrative, dramatic, lyric, or other types of poetry for publication. Attend book launches and publicity events or conduct public readings. Write words to fit musical compositions, including lyrics for operas, musical plays, and choral works. Adapt text to accommodate musical requirements of composers and singers. Teach writing classes. Write humorous material for publication or for performances such as comedy routines, gags, and comedy shows. Collaborate with other writers on specific projects.

Employment Outlook: Projected job growth for these workers stems from increased use of online media and growing demand for Web-based information. But print publishing is expected to continue weakening. Job competition should be keen.

Education of Workforce—Some College: 9.6%. **Associate Degree:** 3.2%. **Bachelor's Degree:** 47.9%. **Master's Degree:** 26.2%. **Doctorate/ Professional Degree:** 9.0%. **Average Age:** 43. **Percentage of Women:** 57.3%.

Skills: Writing; Reading Comprehension; Active Learning; Persuasion; Active Listening; Social Perceptiveness; Negotiation; Complex Problem Solving. **Personality Type(s):** Artistic-Investigative. **Work Environment:** Indoors; sitting; making repetitive motions; using your hands to handle, control, or feel objects, tools, or controls.

Public Relations Specialists

For job description, see Chapter 4.

Reporters and Correspondents

For job description, see Chapter 4.

Technical Writers

- Annual Earnings: $62,730
- Earnings Growth Potential: Medium
- Job Growth: 18.2%
- Annual Job Openings: 1,680
- Self-Employed: 2.0%

Write technical materials, such as equipment manuals, appendixes, or operating and maintenance instructions. May assist in layout work. Organize material and complete writing assignment according to set standards regarding order, clarity, conciseness, style, and terminology. Maintain records and files of work and revisions. Edit, standardize, or make changes to material prepared by other writers or establishment personnel. Confer with customer representatives, vendors, plant executives, or publisher to establish technical specifications and to determine subject material to be developed for publication. Review published materials and recommend revisions or changes in scope, format, content, and methods of reproduction and binding. Select photographs, drawings, sketches, diagrams, and charts to illustrate material. Study drawings, specifications, mockups, and product samples to integrate and delineate technology, operating procedure, and production sequence and detail. Interview production and engineering personnel and read journals and other material to become familiar with product technologies and production methods.

Employment Outlook: Fast growth is expected because of the need for technical writers to explain an increasing number of scientific and technical products. Prospects should be good, especially for workers with strong technical and communication skills. Competition will be keen for some jobs.

Education of Workforce—Some College: 14.1%. **Associate Degree:** 6.1%. **Bachelor's Degree:** 48.9%. **Master's Degree:** 18.8%. **Doctorate/ Professional Degree:** 6.4%. **Average Age:** 46. **Percentage of Women:** No data available.

Skills: Writing; Reading Comprehension; Active Learning; Speaking; Critical Thinking; Complex Problem Solving; Active Listening; Quality Control Analysis. **Personality Type(s):** Artistic-Investigative-Conventional. **Work Environment:** Indoors; sitting; making repetitive motions; using your hands to handle, control, or feel objects, tools, or controls.

CHAPTER 7

The Sales Sequel

Some sales workers start their careers with little or no knowledge of the industry in which they land their first job. In fact, some employers routinely assign management trainees to sales positions, using this work role as the first rung of the corporate ladder. The rationale is that sales work is a good introduction to the business: The worker must learn about the product line and also gets a feel for what the market wants.

However, sales can also be an option as a sequel career. Knowledge of an industry or at least one product can be a great advantage for sales workers.

What Sales Workers Do

The basic function of a sales worker is to convince the buyer that a product or service meets the buyer's needs. That means a good sales worker has a thorough knowledge of the product or service being sold, is able to determine what the buyer's needs are, and has the persuasive skill to sway the buyer to value the benefits of the product or service. As part of the process of closing the sale, the sales worker may need to negotiate the price or at least make the case that the going price is fair. The sales worker also may need to discuss optional features, the mode of delivery, a warranty, or other terms of the deal.

In some companies, the sales manager identifies likely customers by doing research, but sometimes this is done by sales workers. Likewise, an account manager may handle the task of making follow-up phone calls to verify the customer's satisfaction, but often sales workers do this as well. Sometimes sales workers modify the product at the customer's site as needed or train the customer's staff to use the product, but for a highly technical product, this task is more likely to be handled by a sales engineer.

Sales workers usually need to keep track of new products and competition. They may visit trade shows and industry conferences. They attend sales meetings at their company to review their sales performance and learn about current sales goals.

In the table at the end of Chapter 1, you saw the most prominent skills that O*NET lists for the sales occupations. Now, also from O*NET, here are the most important **work activities** that you would do in sales:

- Developing constructive and cooperative working relationships with others and maintaining them over time.

- Convincing others to buy merchandise/goods or to otherwise change their minds or actions.

- Communicating with people outside the organization; representing the organization to customers, the public, government, and other external sources. This information can be exchanged in person, in writing, or by telephone or e-mail.

- Developing specific goals and plans to prioritize, organize, and accomplish your work.

- Observing, receiving, and otherwise obtaining information from all relevant sources.

- Handling complaints, settling disputes, and resolving grievances and conflicts or otherwise negotiating with others.

- Providing information to supervisors, co-workers, and subordinates by telephone, in written form, by e-mail, or in person.

- Identifying information by categorizing, estimating, recognizing differences or similarities, and detecting changes in circumstances or events.

- Keeping up to date technically and applying new knowledge to your job.

- Compiling, coding, categorizing, calculating, tabulating, auditing, or verifying information or data.

The Pros and Cons of Selling

The BLS, surveying seven occupations that are linked to the nine sales jobs included in this chapter, finds average earnings of $54,446, compared to an average of $39,343 for all other occupations. Understand that this average includes the earnings of many workers for whom sales is an entry-level position.

The BLS projects 9.1% growth for the sales occupations from 2008 to 2018 and an average of 16,433 job openings per year.

The O*NET database reports these **work environment** characteristics for sales workers:

- Freedom to Make Decisions
- Structured versus Unstructured Work
- Frequency of Decision Making
- Importance of Being Exact or Accurate
- Impact of Decisions on Co-workers or Company Results
- Time Pressure
- In an Enclosed Vehicle or Equipment
- Level of Competition
- Physical Proximity
- Spend Time Sitting

For working in sales, it helps to have an outgoing personality and be able to get along with many kinds of people. One of the satisfactions of the job is the contact with people, but clients sometimes can be demanding. The work may require a lot of travel. Sales workers are often under pressure to meet a sales quota. Sometimes their income is based partly or wholly on a commission.

How to Move into Sales

Most sales positions have no formal educational requirements. Workers need two kinds of knowledge: knowledge of sales technique and knowledge of the product being sold. Employers may train sales workers in both. For example, a manufacturer may rotate sales trainees among jobs in plants and offices to learn all phases of production, installation, and distribution of the product. Other employers offer formal classes and on-the-job training under the supervision of a field sales manager.

However, a good background in either or both kinds of knowledge will improve your chances of getting hired as well as your success on the job. Employers sometimes recruit sales workers from the end users of their products because these experienced users are familiar with the benefits of the product and the ways to get the best use out of it. Experience like this is particularly valuable for landing a job selling a scientific or technical product, although a bachelor's degree in a scientific or technology field is another way of qualifying for such a job. If you're a knowledgeable user of a product, you might consider approaching the vendor about a sales job.

Sales engineers usually have a bachelor's degree in engineering, but some who hold this job title are knowledgeable about science or technology without being engineers. Usually they learn their skills by being teamed with an experienced sales worker, and they often continue to work as a team with someone who is more skilled with sales technique and less knowledgeable about technology.

Knowledge of a particular industry may give you an advantage in a job selling investments or commodities related to that industry. For jobs selling financial services, securities, or commodities, a bachelor's degree in business, finance, accounting, or economics is important. Sales experience is also valuable but not necessary. Most employers provide intensive on-the-job training, teaching employees the specifics of the firm, such as the products and services offered. Brokers and investment advisors must register as representatives of their firm with the Financial Industry Regulatory Authority (FINRA). Before beginners can qualify as registered representatives, they must be an employee of a registered firm for at least four months and pass the General Securities Registered Representative Examination—known as the Series 7 Exam—administered by FINRA. An MBA degree or certification as a Chartered Financial Analyst can be very valuable for advancement.

The career path for selling insurance is similar. A bachelor's in a business subject is useful, employers train workers on the job, licensure is required, and a certification is useful for advancement. In most states, different licenses are required for each type of insurance, and specific courses are prescribed, as well as continuing education to maintain licensure. Previous technical experience in a particular field can help you get a job selling commercial insurance policies to people in the same profession.

Descriptions of Sales Occupations

The O*NET database includes nine sales occupations that you might consider as sequel careers.

Advertising Sales Agents

- Annual Earnings: $43,360

- Earnings Growth Potential: High

- Job Growth: 7.2%

- Annual Job Openings: 4,510

- Self-Employed: 5.0%

Sell or solicit advertising, including graphic art, advertising space in publications, custom-made signs, or TV and radio advertising time. May obtain leases for outdoor advertising sites or persuade retailer to use sales promotion display items. Maintain assigned account bases while developing new accounts. Explain to customers how specific types of advertising will help promote their products or services in the most effective way possible. Provide clients with estimates of the costs of advertising products or services. Locate and contact potential clients to offer advertising services. Process all correspondence and paperwork related to accounts. Inform customers of available options for advertisement artwork and provide samples. Prepare and deliver sales presentations to new and existing customers to sell new advertising programs and to protect and increase existing advertising. Deliver advertising or illustration proofs to customers for approval. Prepare promotional plans, sales literature, media kits, and sales contracts, using computer. Recommend appropriate sizes and formats for advertising, depending on medium being used. Draw up contracts for advertising work and collect payments due.

Employment Outlook: Continued growth of media outlets is expected to generate demand for advertising sales. Opportunities for entry-level workers should be good, especially for job seekers who have sales experience and a college degree.

Education of Workforce—Some College: 22.5%. **Associate Degree:** 8.6%. **Bachelor's Degree:** 46.0%. **Master's Degree:** 6.6%. **Doctorate/Professional Degree:** 0.6%. **Average Age:** 43. **Percentage of Women:** 27.2%.

Skills: Persuasion; Negotiation; Service Orientation; Speaking; Mathematics; Social Perceptiveness; Systems Evaluation; Systems Analysis. **Personality Type(s):** Enterprising-Conventional-Artistic. **Work Context:** More often indoors than outdoors; sitting; sounds, noisy.

Insurance Sales Agents

- Annual Earnings: $45,500

- Earnings Growth Potential: High

- Job Growth: 11.9%

- Annual Job Openings: 15,260

- Self-Employed: 22.4%

Sell life, property, casualty, health, automotive, or other types of insurance. May refer clients to independent brokers, work as independent broker, or be employed by an insurance company. Sell various types of insurance policies to businesses and individuals on behalf of insurance companies, including automobile, fire, life, property, medical, and dental insurance or specialized policies such as marine, farm/crop, and medical malpractice. Interview prospective clients to obtain data about their financial resources and needs and the physical condition of the person or property to be insured and to discuss any existing coverage. Call on policyholders to deliver and explain policy, to analyze insurance program and suggest additions or changes, or to change beneficiaries. Seek out new clients and develop clientele by networking to find new customers and generate lists of prospective clients. Ensure that policy requirements are fulfilled, including any necessary medical examinations and the completion of appropriate forms. Customize insurance programs to suit individual customers, often covering a variety of risks.

Employment Outlook: Projected employment increases stem from the growth and aging of the population. But these increases will be tempered by insurance carriers attempting to contain costs by relying on independent agents rather than employees. Job opportunities should be best for college graduates with good interpersonal skills.

Education of Workforce—Some College: 26.7%. **Associate Degree:** 9.1%. **Bachelor's Degree:** 37.7%. **Master's Degree:** 6.1%. **Doctorate/ Professional Degree:** 1.4%. **Average Age:** 45. **Percentage of Women:** 55.1%.

Skills: Negotiation; Persuasion; Service Orientation; Active Listening; Systems Analysis; Speaking; Systems Evaluation; Active Learning. **Personality Type(s):** Enterprising-Conventional-Social. **Work Context:** Indoors; sitting.

Sales Agents, Financial Services

- Annual Earnings: $66,930

- Earnings Growth Potential: Very high

- Job Growth: 9.3%

- Annual Job Openings: 12,680

- Self-Employed: 15.4%

Job openings are shared with Sales Agents, Securities and Commodities and with Securities and Commodities Traders.

Sell financial services such as loan, tax, and securities counseling to customers of financial institutions and business establishments. Determine customers' financial services needs and prepare proposals to sell services that address these needs. Contact prospective customers to present information and explain available services. Sell services and equipment, such as trusts, investments, and check processing services. Prepare forms or agreements to complete sales. Develop prospects from current commercial customers, referral leads, and sales and trade meetings. Review business trends in order to advise customers regarding expected fluctuations. Make presentations on financial services to groups to attract new clients. Evaluate costs and revenue of agreements to determine continued profitability.

Employment Outlook: Consolidation of the financial industry is expected to inhibit employment growth. Individuals' ability to manage their own investments online is likely to reduce the need for brokers. Job competition should be keen.

Education of Workforce—Some College: 17.4%. **Associate Degree:** 6.4%. **Bachelor's Degree:** 47.9%. **Master's Degree:** 14.5%. **Doctorate/ Professional Degree:** 2.6%. **Average Age:** 44. **Percentage of Women:** 83.1%.

Skills: Persuasion; Systems Evaluation; Mathematics; Negotiation; Service Orientation; Active Learning; Systems Analysis; Speaking. **Personality Type(s):** Enterprising-Conventional. **Work Context:** Indoors; sitting.

Sales Agents, Securities and Commodities

- Annual Earnings: $66,930

- Earnings Growth Potential: Very high

- Job Growth: 9.3%

- Annual Job Openings: 12,680

- Self-Employed: 15.4%

Job openings are shared with Sales Agents, Financial Services and with Securities and Commodities Traders.

Buy and sell securities in investment and trading firms and develop and implement financial plans for individuals, businesses, and organizations. Complete sales order tickets and submit for processing of client-requested transactions. Interview clients to determine clients' assets, liabilities, cash flow, insurance coverage, tax status, and financial objectives. Record transactions accurately and keep clients informed about transactions. Develop financial plans based on analysis of clients' financial status and discuss financial options with clients. Review all securities transactions to ensure accuracy of information and ensure that trades conform to regulations of governing agencies. Offer advice on the purchase or sale of particular securities. Relay buy or sell orders to securities exchanges or to firm trading departments. Identify potential clients, using advertising campaigns, mailing lists, and personal contacts. Review financial periodicals, stock and bond reports, business publications, and other material to identify potential investments for clients and to keep abreast of trends affecting market conditions.

Employment Outlook: Consolidation of the financial industry is expected to inhibit employment growth. Individuals' ability to manage their own investments online is likely to reduce the need for brokers. Job competition should be keen.

Education of Workforce—Some College: 17.4%. **Associate Degree:** 6.4%. **Bachelor's Degree:** 47.9%. **Master's Degree:** 14.5%. **Doctorate/ Professional Degree:** 2.6%. **Average Age:** 44. **Percentage of Women:** 83.1%.

Skills: Systems Analysis; Persuasion; Systems Evaluation; Management of Financial Resources; Reading Comprehension; Judgment and Decision Making; Service Orientation; Negotiation. **Personality Type(s):** Enterprising-Conventional. **Work Context:** Indoors; sitting.

Sales Engineers

- Annual Earnings: $83,190
- Earnings Growth Potential: High
- Job Growth: 8.8%
- Annual Job Openings: 3,500
- Self-Employed: 0.0%

Sell business goods or services, the selling of which requires a technical background equivalent to a baccalaureate degree in engineering. Plan and modify product configurations to meet customer needs. Confer with customers and engineers to assess equipment needs and to determine system requirements. Collaborate with sales teams to understand customer requirements, to promote the sale of company products, and to provide sales support. Secure and renew orders and arrange delivery. Develop, present, or respond to proposals for specific customer requirements, including request for proposal responses and industry-specific solutions. Sell products requiring extensive technical expertise and support for installation and use, such as material handling equipment, numerical-control machinery, and computer systems. Diagnose problems with installed equipment. Prepare and deliver technical presentations that explain products or services to customers and prospective customers. Recommend improved materials or machinery to customers, documenting how such changes will lower costs or increase production.

Employment Outlook: Projected job growth will stem from the increasing variety and technical nature of goods and services to be sold. Competition is expected. Prospects should be best for job seekers with excellent interpersonal skills and communication, math, and science aptitude.

Education of Workforce—Some College: 15.6%. **Associate Degree:** 8.3%. **Bachelor's Degree:** 54.6%. **Master's Degree:** 14.7%. **Doctorate/ Professional Degree:** 1.0%. **Average Age:** 43. **Percentage of Women:** 5.2%.

Skills: Technology Design; Persuasion; Negotiation; Systems Evaluation; Systems Analysis; Troubleshooting; Active Learning; Judgment and Decision Making. **Personality Type(s):** Enterprising-Realistic-Investigative. **Work Context:** Indoors; sitting; making repetitive motions.

Sales Representatives, Services, All Other

- Annual Earnings: $49,410
- Earnings Growth Potential: High
- Job Growth: 13.9%
- Annual Job Openings: 22,810
- Self-Employed: 3.7%

Job openings are shared with Energy Brokers.

All services sales representatives not listed separately. No task data available.

Employment Outlook: Faster-than-average employment growth is projected.

Education of Workforce—Some College: 25.4%. **Associate Degree:** 8.4%. **Bachelor's Degree:** 38.3%. **Master's Degree:** 7.4%. **Doctorate/ Professional Degree:** 0.8%. **Average Age:** 41. **Percentage of Women:** 16.0%.

Skills: No data available. **Personality Type(s):** No data available. **Work Context:** No data available.

Sales Representatives, Wholesale and Manufacturing, Except Technical and Scientific Products

- Annual Earnings: $50,920

- Earnings Growth Potential: High

- Job Growth: 6.6%

- Annual Job Openings: 45,790

- Self-Employed: 3.7%

Sell goods for wholesalers or manufacturers to businesses or groups of individuals. Work requires substantial knowledge of items sold. Answer customers' questions about products, prices, availability, product uses, and credit terms. Recommend products to customers based on customers' needs and interests. Contact regular and prospective customers to demonstrate products, explain product features, and solicit orders. Estimate or quote prices, credit or contract terms, warranties, and delivery dates. Consult with clients after sales or contract signings to resolve problems and to provide ongoing support. Prepare drawings, estimates, and bids that meet specific customer needs. Provide customers with product samples and catalogs. Identify prospective customers by using business directories, following leads from existing clients, participating in organizations and clubs, and attending trade shows and conferences. Arrange and direct delivery and installation of products and equipment. Monitor market conditions; product innovations; and competitors' products, prices, and sales.

Employment Outlook: Continued expansion in the variety and number of goods sold is expected to lead to additional jobs for these workers. Prospects should be best for job seekers with a college degree, technical expertise, and interpersonal skills.

Education of Workforce—Some College: 23.2%. **Associate Degree:** 8.1%. **Bachelor's Degree:** 39.8%. **Master's Degree:** 6.6%. **Doctorate/ Professional Degree:** 0.7%. **Average Age:** 44. **Percentage of Women:** No data available.

Skills: Negotiation; Persuasion; Service Orientation; Critical Thinking; Operations Analysis; Social Perceptiveness; Active Listening; Speaking. **Personality Type(s):** Conventional-Enterprising. **Work Context:** Outdoors; contaminants; standing; sounds, noisy; sitting; walking and running.

Sales Representatives, Wholesale and Manufacturing, Technical and Scientific Products

- Annual Earnings: $71,340
- Earnings Growth Potential: High
- Job Growth: 9.7%
- Annual Job Openings: 14,230
- Self-Employed: 3.6%

Job openings are shared with Solar Sales Representatives and with Assessors.

Sell goods for wholesalers or manufacturers where technical or scientific knowledge is required in such areas as biology, engineering, chemistry, and electronics that is normally obtained from at least two years of postsecondary education. Contact new and existing customers to discuss their needs and to explain how these needs could be met by specific products and services. Answer customers' questions about products, prices, availability, product uses, and credit terms. Quote prices, credit terms, and other bid specifications. Emphasize product features based on analyses of customers' needs and on technical knowledge of product capabilities and limitations. Negotiate prices and terms of sales and service agreements. Maintain customer records, using automated systems. Identify prospective customers by using business directories, following leads from existing clients, participating in organizations and clubs, and attending trade shows and conferences. Prepare sales contracts for orders obtained and submit orders for processing. Select the correct products or assist customers in making product selections, based on customers' needs, product specifications, and applicable regulations.

Employment Outlook: Continued expansion in the variety and number of goods sold is expected to lead to additional jobs for these workers. Prospects should be best for job seekers with a college degree, technical expertise, and interpersonal skills.

Education of Workforce—Some College: 23.2%. **Associate Degree:** 8.1%. **Bachelor's Degree:** 39.8%. **Master's Degree:** 6.6%. **Doctorate/ Professional Degree:** 0.7%. **Average Age:** 44. **Percentage of Women:** No data available.

Skills: Persuasion; Negotiation; Management of Financial Resources; Management of Material Resources; Active Listening; Speaking; Reading Comprehension; Instructing. **Personality Type(s):** Enterprising-Conventional. **Work Context:** Indoors; sitting.

Securities and Commodities Traders

- Annual Earnings: $66,930

- Earnings Growth Potential: Very high

- Job Growth: 9.3%

- Annual Job Openings: 12,680

- Self-Employed: 27.9%

Job openings are shared with Sales Agents, Financial Services and with Sales Agents, Securities and Commodities.

Buy and sell securities and commodities to transfer debt, capital, or risk. Establish and negotiate unit prices and terms of sale. Buy or sell stocks, bonds, commodity futures, foreign currencies, or other securities at stock exchanges on behalf of investment dealers. Agree on buying or selling prices at optimal levels for clients. Make bids and offers to buy or sell securities. Analyze target companies and investment opportunities to inform investment decisions. Develop and maintain supplier and customer relationships. Devise trading, option, and hedge strategies. Identify opportunities and develop channels for purchase or sale of securities or commodities. Inform other traders, managers, or customers of market conditions, including volume, price, competition, and dynamics. Monitor markets and positions. Process paperwork for special orders, including margin and option purchases. Receive sales order tickets and inspect forms to determine accuracy of information. Report all positions or trading results. Review securities transactions to ensure conformance to regulations. Track and analyze factors that affect price movement, such as trade policies, weather conditions, political developments, and supply-and-demand changes.

Employment Outlook: Consolidation of the financial industry is expected to inhibit employment growth. Individuals' ability to manage their own investments online is likely to reduce the need for brokers. Job competition should be keen.

Education of Workforce—Some College: 17.4%. **Associate Degree:** 6.4%. **Bachelor's Degree:** 47.9%. **Master's Degree:** 14.5%. **Doctorate/ Professional Degree:** 2.6%. **Average Age:** 44. **Percentage of Women:** 15.4%.

Skills: No data available. **Personality Type(s):** Enterprising-Conventional. **Work Context:** No data available.

CHAPTER 8

The Brokerage Sequel

A lot of buying and selling goes on in every industry. Through your work experience, have you become well informed about how these deals get made? That is, do you know who the main sellers are, what they have to offer, how much they're likely to ask in payment, and what makes the difference between a good deal and a bad one? Do you also know about the buyers: where they come from, what they're looking for, what they're able to pay, and what makes the difference between a good customer and a bad one? It would also be useful to know what arrangements besides price are commonly involved in the deal, such as warrantees and common modes of delivery.

If you have all or most of this knowledge, you may be able to make a career of bringing buyers and sellers together and earning a commission on the sales. That is what brokers do.

What Brokers Do

Brokers act as matchmakers. For example, a freight broker finds a business that needs to ship some kind of cargo and matches it with a carrier that can provide the appropriate kind of shipping service at an acceptable price. The freight broker never takes possession of the cargo and merely arranges the deal. The company producing the cargo appreciates the broker's ability to quickly identify a reliable and low-priced shipper. The shipper appreciates the added business, which may result in more trucks plying their routes with full loads.

Brokers often advise and inform buyers to help them make a wise choice and understand the necessary paperwork. For example, a mortgage broker may counsel a borrower on how to correct a situation that harms the borrower's credit rating or may explain the pros and cons of different loan arrangements. An energy broker may explain to a commercial client the benefits and risks of entering a contract with an electric company that locks in a specific rate for electric power for a year.

Some brokers facilitate the sale of a division within a business or even the entire business. Working with a broker in a confidential arrangement keeps news of the planned sale off the street so customers of the business do not lose confidence in it.

In the table at the end of Chapter 1, you saw the most prominent skills that O*NET lists for brokerage occupations. Now, also from O*NET, here are the most important **work activities** that you would do as a broker:

- Developing constructive and cooperative working relationships with others and maintaining them over time.

- Communicating with people outside the organization, representing the organization to customers, the public, government, and other external sources. This information can be exchanged in person, in writing, or by telephone or e-mail.

- Analyzing information and evaluating results to choose the best solution and solve problems.

- Developing specific goals and plans to prioritize, organize, and accomplish your work.

- Performing for people or dealing directly with the public. This includes serving customers in restaurants and stores and receiving clients or guests.

- Keeping up to date technically and applying new knowledge to your job.

- Handling complaints, settling disputes, and resolving grievances and conflicts or otherwise negotiating with others.

- Compiling, coding, categorizing, calculating, tabulating, auditing, or verifying information or data.

- Observing, receiving, and otherwise obtaining information from all relevant sources.

- Convincing others to buy merchandise/goods or to otherwise change their minds or actions.

The Pros and Cons of Brokering

The BLS, in its survey of the 12 occupations linked to the brokerage jobs included in this chapter, finds average earnings of $55,638, compared to an average of $39,328 for all other occupations.

The BLS projects 11.8% growth for the brokerage occupations from 2008 to 2018 and an average of 10,979 job openings per year.

The O*NET database reports these **work environment** characteristics for brokers:

- Importance of Being Exact or Accurate
- Structured versus Unstructured Work
- Frequency of Decision Making
- Freedom to Make Decisions
- Impact of Decisions on Co-workers or Company Results
- Spend Time Sitting
- Indoors, Environmentally Controlled
- Time Pressure
- Level of Competition
- Importance of Repeating Same Tasks

From this list of characteristics, you can see that brokers spend much of their time making decisions. The decisions need to be correct and can have a large impact. The pressure of time and competition can add to the stress of this work. Although brokers have a lot of independence, the context in which they make their decisions tends to be structured and even repetitious. Brokering provides the satisfaction of helping clients achieve their goals. This can be especially rewarding when people can live better lives by achieving goals such as a college degree or the purchase of a home.

How to Move into Brokering

Besides knowledge of an industry, brokers often need to carry insurance to protect their clients from loss. Sometimes they are also required to be bonded, an additional expense when you set up a brokerage.

Knowledge of applicable laws is important in many industries, so it may be necessary for you to take one or more classes to become fully informed and, in many cases, prepare for a licensure exam. (A college degree is rarely necessary, although it can be helpful.) The license assures clients that you know the laws and may also indicate that you possess appropriate insurance. In some industries, a criminal background check is a common requirement. Because there is so much variation, you should check the requirements for your industry and state.

Transportation brokers need to register with the Federal Motor Carrier Safety Administration.

In many industries, a common entry route is to work first as an agent on the staff of a brokerage. Agents usually are not required to carry the level of responsibility, including legal liability, that a broker carries. Licensing and insurance requirements tend to be much lower. (Employment agents are discussed in Chapter 9.) Real estate brokers usually begin as sales agents. In fact, work experience in sales is a requirement for a real estate broker's license, although in some states it is waived for those with a bachelor's degree in real estate.

It's easier to set up a brokerage business in some industries, such as the highly regulated insurance industry, than in others where a few major players dominate.

Descriptions of Brokerage Occupations

The O*NET database includes 12 occupations that work in brokerage. Some of the job titles make them appear to be sales jobs, and in fact some of these also appear in Chapter 7, but the facts that the Department of Labor collects about these occupations also apply to brokers.

Agents and Business Managers of Artists, Performers, and Athletes

- Annual Earnings: $61,890

- Earnings Growth Potential: Very high

- Job Growth: 22.4%

- Annual Job Openings: 1,010

- Self-Employed: 45.8%

Represent and promote artists, performers, and athletes to prospective employers. May handle contract negotiation and other business matters for clients. Manage business and financial affairs for clients, such as arranging travel and lodging, selling tickets, and directing marketing and advertising activities. Obtain information about and/or inspect performance facilities, equipment, and accommodations to ensure that they meet specifications. Negotiate with managers, promoters, union officials, and other persons regarding clients' contractual rights and obligations. Advise clients on financial and legal matters such as investments and taxes. Hire trainers or coaches to advise clients on performance matters such as training techniques or performance presentations. Prepare periodic accounting statements for clients. Keep informed of industry trends and deals. Develop contacts with individuals and organizations and apply effective strategies and techniques to ensure their clients' success. Confer with clients to develop strategies for their careers and to explain actions taken on their behalf.

Employment Outlook: Much-faster-than-average employment growth is projected.

Education of Workforce—Some College: 19.8%. **Associate Degree:** 6.5%. **Bachelor's Degree:** 42.4%. **Master's Degree:** 9.8%. **Doctorate/ Professional Degree:** 4.3%. **Average Age:** 42. **Percentage of Women:** 36.5%.

Skills: Negotiation; Persuasion; Management of Financial Resources; Service Orientation; Judgment and Decision Making; Speaking; Management of Personnel Resources; Time Management. **Personality Type(s):** Enterprising-Social. **Work Context:** Indoors; sitting.

Cargo and Freight Agents

- Annual Earnings: $36,960

- Earnings Growth Potential: Medium

- Job Growth: 23.9%

- Annual Job Openings: 4,030

- Self-Employed: 0.3%

Job openings are shared with Freight Forwarders.

Expedite and route movement of incoming and outgoing cargo and freight shipments in airline, train, and trucking terminals and shipping docks. Take orders from customers and arrange pickup of freight and cargo for delivery to loading platform. Prepare and examine bills of lading to determine shipping charges and tariffs. Negotiate and arrange transport of goods with shipping or freight companies. Notify consignees, passengers, or customers of the arrival of freight or baggage and arrange for delivery. Advise clients on transportation and payment methods. Prepare manifests showing baggage, mail, and freight weights and number of passengers on airplanes and transmit data to destinations. Determine method of shipment and prepare bills of lading, invoices, and other shipping documents. Check import/export documentation to determine cargo contents and classify goods into different fee or tariff groups, using a tariff coding system. Estimate freight or postal rates and record shipment costs and weights. Enter shipping information into a computer by hand or by using a hand-held scanner that reads bar codes on goods. Retrieve stored items and trace lost shipments as necessary. Pack goods for shipping, using tools such as staplers, strapping machines, and hammers.

Employment Outlook: More agents should be needed to handle the growing number of shipments resulting from expected increases in cargo traffic. Job prospects should be good.

Education of Workforce—Some College: 31.1%. **Associate Degree:** 8.8%. **Bachelor's Degree:** 18.3%. **Master's Degree:** 2.3%. **Doctorate/ Professional Degree:** 0.0%. **Average Age:** 43. **Percentage of Women:** No data available.

Skills: Negotiation; Service Orientation; Time Management; Speaking; Persuasion; Critical Thinking; Troubleshooting; Equipment Maintenance. **Personality Type(s):** Conventional-Enterprising-Realistic. **Work Context:** Indoors; sitting; making repetitive motions.

Customs Brokers

- Annual Earnings: $60,610

- Earnings Growth Potential: High

- Job Growth: 11.5%

- Annual Job Openings: 36,830

- Self-Employed: 0.6%

Job openings are shared with Business Continuity Planners; Energy Auditors; Security Management Specialists; and Sustainability Specialists.

Prepare customs documentation and ensure that shipments meet all applicable laws to facilitate the import and export of goods. Determine and track duties and taxes payable and process payments on behalf of client. Sign documents under a power of attorney. Represent clients in meetings with customs officials and apply for duty refunds and tariff reclassifications. Coordinate transportation and storage of imported goods. Sign documents on behalf of clients, using powers of attorney. Provide advice on transportation options, types of carriers, or shipping routes. Post bonds for the products being imported or assist clients in obtaining bonds. Insure cargo against loss, damage, or pilferage. Obtain line releases for frequent shippers of low-risk commodities, high-volume entries, or multiple-container loads. Contract with freight forwarders for destination services. Arrange for transportation, warehousing, or product distribution of imported or exported products. Suggest best methods of packaging or labeling products. Request or compile necessary import documentation, such as customs invoices, certificates of origin, and cargo-control documents. Stay abreast of changes in import or export laws or regulations by reading current literature, attending meetings or conferences, or conferring with colleagues. Quote duty and tax rates on goods to be imported, based on federal tariffs and excise taxes.

Employment Outlook: About-average employment growth is projected.

Education of Workforce—Some College: 23.1%. **Associate Degree:** 11.6%. **Bachelor's Degree:** 32.3%. **Master's Degree:** 12.9%. **Doctorate/ Professional Degree:** 2.7%. **Average Age:** 44. **Percentage of Women:** No data available.

Skills: No data available. **Personality Type(s):** Enterprising-Conventional. **Work Context:** No data available.

Energy Brokers

- Annual Earnings: $49,410

- Earnings Growth Potential: High

- Job Growth: 13.9%

- Annual Job Openings: 22,810

- Self-Employed: 3.7%

Job openings are shared with Sales Representatives, Services, All Other.

Purchase or sell energy for customers. Contact prospective buyers or sellers of power to arrange transactions. Create product packages based on assessment of customers' or potential customers' needs. Educate customers and answer customer questions related to the buying or selling of energy, energy markets, or alternative energy sources. Explain contracts and related documents to customers. Forecast energy supply and demand to minimize the cost of meeting load demands and to maximize the value of supply resources. Negotiate prices and contracts for energy sales or purchases. Price energy based on market conditions. Analyze customer bills and utility rate structures to select optimal rate structures for customers. Develop and deliver proposals or presentations on topics such as the purchase and sale of energy. Facilitate the delivery or receipt of wholesale power or retail load scheduling. Monitor the flow of energy in response to changes in consumer demand.

Employment Outlook: Faster-than-average employment growth is projected.

Education of Workforce—Some College: 25.4%. **Associate Degree:** 8.4%. **Bachelor's Degree:** 38.3%. **Master's Degree:** 7.4%. **Doctorate/ Professional Degree:** 0.8%. **Average Age:** 41. **Percentage of Women:** No data available.

Skills: No data available. **Personality Type(s):** Enterprising-Conventional. **Work Context:** No data available.

Insurance Sales Agents

For job description, see Chapter 7.

Investment Underwriters

- Annual Earnings: $58,350

- Earnings Growth Potential: Medium

- Job Growth: 10.5%

- Annual Job Openings: 4,320

- Self-Employed: 0.9%

Job openings are shared with Financial Quantitative Analysts; Fraud Examiners, Investigators and Analysts; and Risk Management Specialists.

Intermediate between corporate issuers of securities and clients regarding private equity investments. Underwrite the issuance of securities to provide capital for client growth. Negotiate and structure the terms of mergers and acquisitions. Structure marketing campaigns to find buyers for new securities. Supervise, train, or mentor junior team members. Assess companies as investments for clients by examining company facilities. Prepare all materials for transactions and execution of deals. Perform securities valuation and pricing. Determine desirability of deals to develop solutions to financial problems or to assess the financial and capital impact of transactions, using financial modeling. Develop and maintain client relationships. Evaluate capital needs of clients and assess market conditions to inform structuring of financial packages. Create client presentations of plan details. Coordinate due diligence processes and the negotiation and execution of purchase and sale agreements. Collaborate on projects with teams of other professionals, such as lawyers, accountants, and public relations experts. Confer with clients to restructure debt, refinance debt, or raise new debt.

Employment Outlook: About-average employment growth is projected.

Education of Workforce—Some College: 21.1%. **Associate Degree:** 10.0%. **Bachelor's Degree:** 34.1%. **Master's Degree:** 13.9%. **Doctorate/ Professional Degree:** 2.9%. **Average Age:** 42. **Percentage of Women:** No data available.

Skills: No data available. **Personality Type(s):** Conventional-Enterprising. **Work Context:** No data available.

Loan Officers

- Annual Earnings: $54,880

- Earnings Growth Potential: High

- Job Growth: 10.1%

- Annual Job Openings: 6,880

- Self-Employed: 3.7%

Evaluate, authorize, or recommend approval of commercial, real estate, or credit loans. Advise borrowers on financial status and methods of payments. Includes mortgage loan officers and agents, collection analysts, loan servicing officers, and loan underwriters. Meet with applicants to obtain information for loan applications and to answer questions about the process. Approve loans within specified limits and refer loan applications outside those limits to management for approval. Analyze applicants' financial status, credit, and property evaluations to determine feasibility of granting loans. Explain to customers the different types of loans and credit options that are available, as well as the terms of those services. Obtain and compile copies of loan applicants' credit histories, corporate financial statements, and other financial information. Review and update credit and loan files. Review loan agreements to ensure that they are complete and accurate according to policy. Compute payment schedules. Stay abreast of new types of loans and other financial services and products to better meet customers' needs. Submit applications to credit analysts for verification and recommendation.

Employment Outlook: Overall economic expansion and population growth are expected to increase employment of these workers. However, increased automation through the use of the Internet loan application will temper employment growth. Good job opportunities are expected.

Education of Workforce—Some College: 25.5%. **Associate Degree:** 10.1%. **Bachelor's Degree:** 39.5%. **Master's Degree:** 7.5%. **Doctorate/ Professional Degree:** 0.9%. **Average Age:** 42. **Percentage of Women:** 58.0%.

Skills: Mathematics; Service Orientation; Speaking; Operations Analysis; Writing; Judgment and Decision Making; Reading Comprehension; Active Listening. **Personality Type(s):** Conventional-Enterprising-Social. **Work Context:** Indoors; sitting; making repetitive motions.

Purchasing Agents and Buyers, Farm Products

- Annual Earnings: $53,150

- Earnings Growth Potential: High

- Job Growth: −1.1%

- Annual Job Openings: 310

- Self-Employed: 8.5%

Purchase farm products for further processing or resale. Coordinate and direct activities of workers engaged in cutting, transporting, storing, or milling products and in maintaining records. Maintain records of business transactions and product inventories, reporting data to companies or government agencies as necessary. Sell supplies such as seed, feed, fertilizers, and insecticides, arranging for loans or financing as necessary. Estimate land production possibilities, surveying property and studying factors such as crop rotation history, soil fertility, and irrigation facilities. Negotiate contracts with farmers for the production or purchase of farm products. Review orders to determine product types and quantities required to meet demand. Examine and test crops and products to estimate their value, determine their grade, and locate any evidence of disease or insect damage. Arrange for transportation and/or storage of purchased products. Arrange for processing and/or resale of purchased products.

Employment Outlook: Almost all of the growth is expected to be for purchasing agents, except wholesale, retail, and farm products, as more companies demand a greater number of goods and services.

Education of Workforce—Some College: 20.8%. **Associate Degree:** 10.6%. **Bachelor's Degree:** 22.2%. **Master's Degree:** 1.2%. **Doctorate/ Professional Degree:** 0.9%. **Average Age:** 49. **Percentage of Women:** No data available.

Skills: Management of Financial Resources; Management of Material Resources; Persuasion; Negotiation; Management of Personnel Resources; Mathematics; Speaking; Critical Thinking. **Personality Type(s):** Enterprising-Conventional-Realistic. **Work Context:** Indoors; sitting.

Purchasing Agents, Except Wholesale, Retail, and Farm Products

- Annual Earnings: $54,810
- Earnings Growth Potential: Medium
- Job Growth: 13.9%
- Annual Job Openings: 11,860
- Self-Employed: 1.4%

Purchase machinery, equipment, tools, parts, supplies, or services necessary for the operation of an establishment. Purchase raw or semi-finished materials for manufacturing. Purchase the highest quality merchandise at the lowest possible price and in correct amounts. Prepare purchase orders, solicit bid proposals, and review requisitions for goods and services. Research and evaluate suppliers based on price, quality, selection, service, support, availability, reliability, production and distribution capabilities, and the supplier's reputation and history. Analyze price proposals, financial reports, and other data and information to determine reasonable prices. Monitor and follow applicable laws and regulations. Negotiate or renegotiate and administer contracts with suppliers, vendors, and other representatives. Monitor shipments to ensure that goods come in on time, and in the event of problems, trace shipments and follow up undelivered goods. Confer with staff, users, and vendors to discuss defective or unacceptable goods or services and determine corrective action.

Employment Outlook: Almost all of the growth is expected to be for purchasing agents, except wholesale, retail, and farm products, as more companies demand a greater number of goods and services.

Education of Workforce—Some College: 27.9%. **Associate Degree:** 10.8%. **Bachelor's Degree:** 30.0%. **Master's Degree:** 7.6%. **Doctorate/ Professional Degree:** 0.9%. **Average Age:** 45. **Percentage of Women:** 56.5%.

Skills: Management of Financial Resources; Negotiation; Monitoring; Persuasion; Judgment and Decision Making; Speaking; Writing; Systems Evaluation. **Personality Type(s):** Conventional-Enterprising. **Work Context:** Indoors; sitting; using your hands to handle, control, or feel objects, tools, or controls; making repetitive motions.

Real Estate Brokers

- Annual Earnings: $55,740

- Earnings Growth Potential: Very high

- Job Growth: 8.6%

- Annual Job Openings: 3,080

- Self-Employed: 58.3%

Operate real estate office or work for commercial real estate firm, overseeing real estate transactions. Other duties usually include selling real estate or renting properties and arranging loans. Sell, for a fee, real estate owned by others. Obtain agreements from property owners to place properties for sale with real estate firms. Monitor fulfillment of purchase contract terms to ensure that they are handled in a timely manner. Compare a property with similar properties that have recently sold to determine its competitive market price. Act as an intermediary in negotiations between buyers and sellers over property prices and settlement details and during the closing of sales. Generate lists of properties for sale, their locations and descriptions, and available financing options, using computers. Maintain knowledge of real estate law; local economies; fair housing laws; and types of available mortgages, financing options, and government programs. Check work completed by loan officers, attorneys, and other professionals to ensure that it is performed properly. Arrange for financing of property purchases. Appraise property values, assessing income potential when relevant.

Employment Outlook: A growing population is expected to require the services of real estate agents and brokers, creating more jobs for these workers. People who are well trained, ambitious, and socially and professionally active in their communities should have the best prospects.

Education of Workforce—Some College: 28.4%. **Associate Degree:** 9.6%. **Bachelor's Degree:** 34.6%. **Master's Degree:** 8.5%. **Doctorate/Professional Degree:** 2.0%. **Average Age:** 49. **Percentage of Women:** 54.4%.

Skills: Negotiation; Persuasion; Judgment and Decision Making; Active Learning; Speaking; Reading Comprehension; Service Orientation; Active Listening. **Personality Type(s):** Enterprising-Conventional. **Work Context:** More often indoors than outdoors; sitting.

Sales Agents, Financial Services

For job description, see Chapter 7.

Securities and Commodities Traders

- Annual Earnings: $66,930
- Earnings Growth Potential: Very high
- Job Growth: 9.3%
- Annual Job Openings: 12,680
- Self-Employed: 15.4%

Job openings are shared with Sales Agents, Financial Services and with Sales Agents, Securities and Commodities.

Buy and sell securities and commodities to transfer debt, capital, or risk. Establish and negotiate unit prices and terms of sale. Agree on buying or selling prices at optimal levels for clients. Buy or sell stocks, bonds, commodity futures, foreign currencies, or other securities at stock exchanges on behalf of investment dealers. Make bids and offers to buy or sell securities. Analyze target companies and investment opportunities to inform investment decisions. Develop and maintain supplier and customer relationships. Devise trading, option, and hedge strategies. Identify opportunities and develop channels for purchase or sale of securities or commodities. Inform other traders, managers, or customers of market conditions, including volume, price, competition, and dynamics. Monitor markets and positions. Process paperwork for special orders, including margin and option purchases. Receive sales order tickets and inspect forms to determine accuracy of information. Report all positions or trading results. Review securities transactions to ensure conformance to regulations.

Employment Outlook: Consolidation of the financial industry is expected to inhibit employment growth. Individuals' ability to manage their own investments online is likely to reduce the need for brokers. Job competition should be keen.

Education of Workforce—Some College: 17.4%. **Associate Degree:** 6.4%. **Bachelor's Degree:** 47.9%. **Master's Degree:** 14.5%. **Doctorate/ Professional Degree:** 2.6%. **Average Age:** 44. **Percentage of Women:** 27.9%.

Skills: No data available. **Personality Type(s):** Enterprising-Conventional. **Work Context:** No data available.

CHAPTER 9

Other Sequels

The previous seven chapters do not exhaust all the possible ways you can use your work experience in a new career. This chapter features a grab-bag of comparatively small sequel careers. Each one is associated with a small number of workers but still deserves your consideration, if only to drive home the point that your knowledge can be the key to many new career options.

Be sure to read the last section of this chapter for ideas about how to discover other sequel careers.

The Recruitment and Agency Sequels

Every business needs to find new talent, but hiring is one of the hardest parts of a manager's job. Even in a recession, it can be difficult to find appropriately skilled workers who are affordable and will be a good fit for the organization.

Here's where you may play a role. Through your work experience, you may have a good understanding of what sort of person is successful in your industry. You may know which schools and colleges produce graduates with the most appropriate skills. You may even have personal contacts at some of these schools or at companies where workers may be willing to jump ship.

You've heard of the sports scouts who go out looking for athletic talent. Why not do the same thing for other kinds of businesses? Recruiters from corporations and large government agencies visit college campuses to interview prospective entry-level employees. These workers are usually fairly low in the hierarchy of the human resources department, so this is not likely to be something you would seek as a sequel career. However, another kind of recruiter seeks department heads and other highly skilled and experienced workers. These high-level recruiters, commonly referred to as headhunters, often run their own business, earning a commission for each successful placement. Your knowledge of your industry, combined with skill at persuasion, might enable you to be successful in this role.

A related worker is the employment agent. Again, the sports world offers a familiar example: the agent who represents talented athletes and handles negotiations with the teams that want to hire them. You've also heard about agents who represent show business performers. In the business world, employment agents collect fees when they find work for project managers, computer systems analysts, writers, and other highly skilled workers, especially those who work on a project-by-project basis. Short-term workers constantly need to find their next job but may be too wrapped up in their high-pressure projects to be able to spend time making connections with employers. That's why they hire agents who are knowledgeable about the industry and know where to find the next job opening. Agents in sports and show business often have law degrees because so much money is at stake and the legal agreements are often very complex, with clauses that deal with residuals, product endorsements, the possibility of injuries, and so forth. In the business world, that professional background is often not needed. Laurie Harper, an agent for nonfiction writers, says that a good way to learn the skills for her job is to work for a year or less as an intern or assistant in a literary agency. It also helps to read how-to-get-published books and magazines aimed at writers. You'd do something similar to get started as an agent in another field.

Many employment agents operate or work in companies that place consultants in assignments. Under this arrangement, the place of business where the skilled professional actually works does not pay that worker directly. Instead, the agency hires and pays the professional (including fringe benefits), and the agency is paid by the place of business. Businesses appreciate the flexibility that this arrangement provides because they can more easily acquire and get rid of workers than through the conventional hiring relationship. This form of work is recognized as an industry by the Department of Labor, which projects it to grow faster than any other major industry.

The New Product Development Sequel

Nowadays, many new products are technological, so you may think that they are developed mainly by engineers. Actually, teams of workers from several different backgrounds come together to collaborate on the development of most new products. Even if the product is an electronic gadget, the new product development (NPD) team often includes not only engineers, but also marketing managers, technical writers, artists, commercial designers, logistics specialists, cost estimators, and perhaps even anthropologists. Each kind of worker on the team brings different skills that contribute to the success of the new product.

The task of the NPD manager is making all of these elements come together effectively. NPD management is similar in many ways to starting up a new business, and in fact many entrepreneurs build their businesses on new products. (See the following discussion of the entrepreneurial sequel.) That's also why large companies sometimes spin off a daughter company (sometimes called a "skunk works") for NPD efforts: It allows creative workers to hatch new product ideas outside of the normal corporate environment. Besides creativity, NPD requires workers to reach out beyond their narrow specializations and collaborate with other specialists. When this succeeds, everyone in the team learns new work habits and contributes insights to teammates from other disciplines. Good NPD strategies are useful in almost every industry.

Instead of waiting for a manager to ask you to join an NPD team, you can devise a new product idea and convince a manager that it has potential. You can strengthen your case by getting buy-in from workers in other disciplines. For example, if you can get an engineer to agree that the idea is technically feasible and a marketer to agree that buyers might welcome the product, you may get a green light for taking your proposal through the next steps—first for crafting a formal business plan and eventually for undertaking development.

The Entrepreneurial Sequel

Entrepreneurs start and run their own business. In many ways, this sequel overlaps with the management sequel. Entrepreneurs have to manage the beginning of their business, although they may turn over management to someone else once the business becomes established.

Getting a business started involves some special managerial responsibilities: finding an unmet need, devising a way to meet that need, getting financial backing, assembling the resources to produce the product or service, and making first contacts in the market.

The Department of Labor does not provide a separate job description for entrepreneurs because this work function can be regarded as one way of pursuing any of numerous different occupations. In fact, you can pursue *any* of the sequels included in this book as an entrepreneur.

Being an entrepreneur requires originality, a lot of drive, and a willingness to take risks. The Small Business Administration estimates that about half of new businesses do not survive beyond five years. For this reason, many people who try entrepreneurship are comparatively young. Young people tend to have fewer commitments to family that would divide their energies and less to lose if the business goes belly-up. They may have fresher ideas than older workers and a better understanding of emerging technologies and what will appeal to the youth market.

On the other hand, experienced workers bring other strengths to an entre-preneurial career. They have industry knowledge and contacts that are useful in all the different sequel careers described in this book. The oldest of them may have a nest egg saved up and no mortgage or children's col-lege fund demanding payments. Sometimes they have few other choices. If employers are reluctant to hire them because of age discrimination, they may find that the best way to continue their present occupation or pursue a sequel career is to do it in a business of their own.

Most businesses require some level of investment to get started, and unless you personally have the necessary funds, you'll need to convince a banker or other investors to finance your startup. That requires a business plan, in which you spell out what product or service you intend to offer and how you will produce it, find a market for it, and distribute it. Guy Kawasaki, who has written several books about entrepreneurship, emphasizes that you need to be able to explain in 30 seconds what your company does.

You may need an office or production facilities and workers with appropriate skills. Sometimes a license, permit, or insurance is necessary. You may want to plan for how you will scale up the business if it is successful. These considerations are just a brief overview of the concerns that entrepreneurs have to address.

Keep in mind that some entrepreneurial efforts are not aimed at making anybody rich. You may want to start a not-for-profit business that advances a social, environmental, educational, political, or other goal that you consider important. The success of such a venture will depend on your ability to attract charitable donations or to sell products or services on a break-even basis. One way to do this as a sequel career is to leverage your knowledge and contacts within your industry to start an industry association. Although most industries already have organizations in place, there is room for specialized new groups—for example, to deal with green issues.

The Management Analyst Sequel

As business becomes more complex, firms are continually faced with new challenges. They increasingly rely on management analysts to help them remain competitive amidst these changes. Management analysts, often referred to as *business analysts* or *management consultants* in private industry, analyze and propose ways to improve an organization's structure, efficiency, or profits.

For example, a small but rapidly growing company might employ a consultant who is an expert in just-in-time inventory management to help improve its inventory-control system. In another case, a large company that has recently acquired a new division may hire management analysts to help reorganize the corporate structure and eliminate duplicate or nonessential jobs. In recent years, information technology and electronic commerce have provided new opportunities for management analysts with experience in those fields.

Management analysts usually divide their time between their offices and the client's site. That means they travel frequently. They also may need to do unpaid overtime work and may experience a lot of stress when trying to meet a client's demands, often on a tight schedule.

Although this is a popular job among college graduates with business degrees, usually as employees of consulting firms, many workers enter this field as a way of leveraging years of work experience—perhaps after retirement or after being laid off from a salaried position. About one-quarter of management analysts are self-employed.

Employment of management analysts is expected to grow 24 percent, much faster than the average for all occupations. Despite projected rapid employment growth, keen competition is expected for jobs as management analysts because the independent and challenging nature of the work and the high earnings potential make this occupation attractive to many.

The Forensic Sequel

Forensic work takes place in the justice system. It helps prosecutors establish guilt in criminal cases and helps litigators gauge liability in civil cases. It also helps defense lawyers make their cases. (Legal interpreting and translating are covered in Chapter 6.)

Many forensic jobs are entry-level specializations within an occupation, something that people can aim for at the beginning of a career. For example, many forensic scientists prepare by getting a master's degree in that field directly after earning their bachelor's degree in a science, such as forensic science, chemistry, biology, or physics. They aid criminal investigations by drawing conclusions scientifically from bullet fragments, blood spatter patterns, chemical residues, insect traces, and other bits of crime scene evidence. (It's more a behind-the-scenes lab science than what gets portrayed on TV.)

On the other hand, particularly in nonscientific fields, workers often move into forensic work as a sequel career. In fact, you may be surprised at how many different types of workers can apply their knowledge and skills to criminal investigations and court cases. Here's a partial list, with examples of the work they do:

Occupation Title	Example of Forensic Work They Do
Accountants	Find evidence of fraud and embezzlement in financial records.
Anthropologists	Identify the sex and age of a person from skeletal remains.
Artists	Construct a model of a face from skeletal remains.
Biologists	Match DNA from a suspect to DNA found at a crime scene.
Chemists	Identify the likely source of a polluting substance in a waterway.
Computer Scientists	Retrieve supposedly erased documents and e-mail messages as evidence.
Dentists	Identify a person by comparing teeth to dental records.
Economists	Calculate appropriate damages when people sue.
Engineers	Determine cause of failure of a structure so liability can be assigned.
Photographers	Photograph a crime scene from multiple angles.
Physicists	Reconstruct events in a car crash from physical evidence.
Psychologists	Assess a defendant's competency to stand trial.
Registered Nurses	Care for a victim of sexual assault and collect evidence.
Science Technicians	Match a bullet to a weapon.

Some other workers who play forensic roles (mainly as expert witnesses) are astronomers, genealogists, linguists, meteorologists, and social workers.

Many workers do forensic tasks as a sideline or as a specialization within their existing job rather than as an essentially new job. For example, it's unlikely that you could make a full-time sequel career of forensic astronomy. You might occasionally testify in court about issues such as the size of a shadow that will be thrown by a proposed skyscraper, but such cases are rare.

The amount of formal training required to specialize in forensics varies among these occupations. In the sciences, a specialized master's degree is usually required. For nurses, a master's or certification would be appropriate. Forensic engineers need to be licensed and sometimes get a master's degree.

Your opportunities in this field will be limited at best if you have a criminal record.

How to Discover Other Sequel Careers

The lesson to take away from this chapter is that the number of possible sequel careers is limited only by your imagination.

Could you *appraise* the value of some item that you're very knowledgeable about? Could you *advise investors* about its future value? On the basis of your work experience, could your help insurers *estimate risks* within your industry? Are you knowledgeable about *common security threats and countermeasures* in your industry? Do you know how to guard against the most common *fraudulent practices?* Do you know how to *recover from disasters* that are typical of the industry? Could you *estimate costs* for proposed projects? Could you get good deals making *purchases* of merchandise or services? Could you provide *career advice* for people interested in your industry? On the basis of contacts or work experience in another country, could you start an *import-export* business or advise an American company on doing business there?

Any work activity that goes on in your industry may be a sequel career for you, provided you have the interest and the particular skills that this work role requires. Think about work roles in your industry that you are not filling now. Think about needs that are not being met. What work roles could you do better than the people who are doing them now?

Next, think about *other* industries that can benefit from your accumulated knowledge. You've seen how teaching is an example of this: taking knowledge you acquired in your present industry and using it in the education industry. Forensic work is another example; here, the justice system benefits from your expertise.

Another resource that may be useful is a site provided by the U.S. Department of Labor, mySkills myFuture (www.myskillsmyfuture.org). At this site, you enter the name of a current or previous job, and it retrieves a list of occupations with similar skill and knowledge requirements. Some of these occupations may be worth considering as sequel careers. (The site also offers links to detailed information about the job titles it retrieves.)

But be sure not to limit your thinking to traditional job titles. At this stage of your career, your personal mix of knowledge, skills, and interests probably equips you to work in some job function that doesn't fit neatly into conventional lists of occupations. My official job title is Senior Product Developer; I might also be described as a Career Information Writer. Neither of these titles appears in O*NET or in any other list of job titles I've ever seen.

When you think about work you might do, use your imagination. There's a sequel waiting to be staged, with you in the starring role.

CHAPTER 10

Preview Your Sequel Career

You've learned about some common types of sequel careers in the previous chapters. Now it's time for you to decide which sequel career is right for you.

Doing Additional Research

This book's profiles of sequel careers are very brief. There simply isn't enough room here to give lengthy descriptions. But before you commit to a career, you need to have a clear picture of what you're getting into. Following are some resources for learning more about any career you're considering.

Start by reading more about the sequel careers that interest you. Here are some particularly helpful resources:

- The O*NET site of the Department of Labor is a major source of the information in this book. For additional details from this database, go to http://online.onetcenter.org.

- The *Occupational Outlook Handbook* is a vital source of information about careers—and not just about their outlook. You can find it online at www.bls.gov/oco, and JIST publishes a print version with additional exclusive content.

- The Department of Labor's Career OneStop site, www.careeronestop.org, has detailed O*NET data and also wage and outlook information for your state.

The Toe-in-the-Water Approach

There's a limit to how much anybody can learn about careers from reading. You also should explore sequel careers through experiences. Experiences can be very vivid and can allow you to explore the issues that matter most to you.

First-hand experience with a possible sequel career has two advantages:

- It helps you confirm that this sequel suits you.
- It gets you work experience that will be helpful when you seek a job in the sequel career.

However, experiences are time-consuming compared to reading. That's why you generally want to use experiential learning after you have narrowed down your choices to a small number. You also can save time by limiting your experiences to small samples of the career options that interest you. Stick your toe in the water and then decide whether you want to take the full plunge.

Some useful strategies for the toe-in-the-water approach are **getting an experimental job assignment, doing the work as a sideline,** and **doing the work as a volunteer**.

Getting an Experimental Job Assignment

In this strategy, your goal is to take on some of the functions of the sequel career as part of your present job.

For example, if the sequel you have in mind is teaching, take on training a new co-worker. For sales, take on some small aspect of the sales effort, such as researching likely customers.

Here's how to get started: E-mail the following message to your boss, after filling in the blank. For ideas for what to put in the blank, turn to the table at the end of Chapter 1 and look at the skills that are listed for the sequel career you have in mind. Or look at the work activities listed in the chapter that describes the sequel career. Go ahead and play around with the wording in the rest of the message if you like, but try to cover all of the major points. If you'd rather not use e-mail to get this message across, you may use the ideas as the basis for a conversation with your boss. In a conversation, your boss may be able to suggest a role where you'd be most helpful.

E-mail That Requests a Skill-Testing Assignment

I have been working on improving my _____ skill and would really appreciate some feedback from you regarding this skill. I believe a good way for me to get this feedback is to tackle a work task that requires this skill at a level beyond what you've seen me do in the past. If I handle the task correctly and demonstrate the skill, please let me know I've done so. If I make any mistakes, I want to know about them, too. Please let me know not just what I've done wrong, but how I can do the task better. I promise I won't be defensive about your comments.

I'm not asking for extra pay for doing this, and doing it would not imply I've been promoted or have changed departments. I also assure you that I won't let this extra task interfere with my usual work assignments. If necessary, I'll work on this task outside of my regular work hours.

Please give some thought to what task would be appropriate—a challenge, but not so difficult that I'm guaranteed to fail. If you're not sure, I can suggest some possible tasks that you can choose from. I'll be happy to answer any other questions you have about this experiment.

Keep in mind that this experiment exposes you to only a small taste of the sequel career. You may want to engage in more than one such experiment to confirm that the sequel career interests you and that you have some mastery of the various skills it requires.

After your work in this assignment has achieved some positive results, be sure to revise your resume to reflect what you've done and the skills you've demonstrated. Also, when you're up for a performance appraisal, remind your boss of these achievements.

Before you make a request of this kind, it's a good idea to consider how your manager is likely to react. The request implies that you are considering a change in your work role—possibly even a new job. Some managers will welcome your desire for a more fulfilling job. Others will feel threatened by the possibility of losing you or facing competition from you. So try to open a conversation with your manager about the possible directions your career might take. You may learn about opportunities that you weren't aware of, or you may find that this strategy is not advisable because your manager doesn't want you to change your work role in any way.

If this strategy is not an option, you still have two other strategies you can use to test the waters.

Doing the Work as a Sideline

You can try out many of the sequel careers as moonlighting activities. For example, blogging can be a way to refine your communications or advocacy skills. You can practice your teaching skills as a tutor.

If you can't get hired for a part-time job in the field of your sequel, it may be easier for you to start your own small business. With success, you may decide to pursue the entrepreneurial sequel, or you may leverage your experience by getting hired. For example, let's say you have worked for many years as a technician who services swimming pools. You are aware of a certain article of clothing or equipment that technicians like you would find useful but that isn't well known. You could set up a small business buying these items from a supplier and selling them to other technicians, starting with your co-workers and expanding to others in the industry. Eventually, you might expand your product line and make this activity a regular business (the entrepreneurial sequel). Or your demonstrated ability to get products sold might convince someone to hire you as a sales worker (the sales sequel) or a sales or marketing manager (the management sequel). It's even conceivable that the real strength of your sales might be the slickness of your catalog, which might open the door for you to work in a communications sequel.

If you use this strategy, be careful not to choose an activity that will compete in any way with the business of your regular employer. Competitive activity will endanger your day job and may violate your terms of employment, exposing you to the risk of a lawsuit. Also, don't let your moonlighting work spill over into your day job. Your boss expects you to devote your workday to the job you were hired for.

Doing the Work as a Volunteer

It's not necessary for you to be paid while you try out a new work role. You can gain experience doing sequel-related work as a volunteer. Several chapters in this book point out specific volunteer activities you can do to sample a sequel career and chalk up accomplishments that can find a place on your resume.

Volunteer organizations are always looking for willing workers. In most cases, you don't need to be a dues-paying member of long standing to offer your services. In fact, most organizations are pleased and impressed by new members who come through the door with their sleeves rolled up.

Here's a script for a phone call you can make to an organization to offer your services as a volunteer. Fill in the blanks for an appropriate volunteer activity and a related activity for which you already have experience. You probably want to use a lot of your own wording rather than repeating this on the phone word-for-word. But try to mention all of the important points included here.

Phone Script for an Offer to Volunteer

Hello. I understand that you need volunteers to do _____.
I'd be glad to do this for your organization. I should point out right away that I don't have much experience doing _____, but I'm really eager to learn how. I do have some experience doing a related task, _____, so I should be able to learn this new task if someone shows me how. Probably the best way to start is for you to team me up with an experienced volunteer. I promise I'll try very hard to get up to speed quickly.

When would be a good time to get started?

The particular type of organization you might consider depends partly on the sequel career you have in mind and partly on what's available in your community. (If you're highly motivated, you could even start up a new organization.) Consider a charitable fund-raising campaign, a faith group, a fraternal organization, a civic group, a business association, a women's shelter, a political campaign, an environmentalist group, a food pantry, an arts group, a sports league, a team's booster club, a parent-teacher organization, an animal shelter, a hobbyists' or crafters' group, a literacy-tutoring program, a walking-tour group, a community safety patrol, or a museum-support group.

Remember that most volunteer groups need workers for roles that are not part of their central mission but rather are supporting functions. For example, environmentalist groups need volunteers to write publicity; political campaigns need volunteers to maintain their database of likely voters. Often you can find a role that helps you build a skill for your sequel career even though the mission of the volunteer organization has little to do with the industry where you want to stage your sequel.

CHAPTER 11

Stage Your Sequel Career

It's never too early to start researching job openings. Even if you're still undecided about your sequel career goal, you should find out about job opportunities in the community where you want to live and work. Why waste your time, money, and energy preparing for a career that has few job openings? If you're going to need to relocate to find work in your chosen field, isn't it better to know that now?

On the other hand, maybe you're much further along in the career-planning process. Maybe you've already made up your mind about your sequel career goal. You may even have completed any expected entry requirements, so you're ready to apply for a job in your targeted occupation. But before you put on your job-interview clothes, you need to learn how to conduct a job search.

Preparing for the Job Hunt

Big-game hunters always bring the right weapons and ammo, and sequel-job hunters also need to gear up for their efforts. To start, you need to have your resume in good shape so you can send it off on short notice. The resume needs to show a tight focus on the kind of job you want and the strengths you bring to the employer. The cover letter also should be based on this focused thinking.

This book does not have room for examples of resumes and cover letters, but here are some helpful JIST books about these documents:

- *Résumé Magic: Trade Secrets of a Professional Resume Writer,* by Susan Britton Whitcomb

- *Cover Letter Magic: Trade Secrets of Professional Resume Writers,* by Wendy S. Enelow and Louise M. Kursmark

- *30-Minute Resume Makeover*, by Louise M. Kursmark

- *Amazing Resumes,* by Jim Bright, Ph.D., and Joanne Earl, Ph.D.

Another tool in your job-hunting kit is the "elevator speech," which you should prepare and rehearse before you start pursuing job leads. This is a brief statement of who you are, what kind of job you're seeking, and why you qualify for this kind of job. No matter where you use this speech, it must be concise enough that you could say it to someone on an elevator and get all your points across before the elevator has stopped.

Finding the Hidden Jobs

You may have already heard about the "hidden job market." Studies have revealed that most jobs are found not by answering an advertisement in a newspaper or by waiting for a website to match you to an employer, but rather through personal contacts.

There are two basic strategies for finding out about unadvertised jobs: **cold-calling** employers who hire people for the kind of job you have in mind and **networking** so that you hear about potential job openings. The two overlap to some extent: Through a cold call to an employer, you may hear about a possible job elsewhere, and through your network, you may hear about employers who are most likely to be worth cold-calling. You can pursue both strategies simultaneously.

Both networking and cold-calling require you to move outside your comfort zone. Your problem is that you don't know about the hidden job openings. You won't learn about them by talking only to your friends, because your friends tend to know most of the same things you know. The principle behind networking is that by connecting to *the people your friends know,* you can learn information (in this case, about jobs) that ordinarily would not be available to you. The principle behind cold-calling is that by talking directly to *the people who make hiring decisions,* you can learn about jobs that may never be advertised.

Networking

In networking, the usual procedure is to make a list of everyone you know, call them, give them your elevator speech, and make clear to them what sort of work you're looking for. You may also find it useful to ask them for advice and look on this as a final stage of career exploration. For example, you might ask them what businesses need people like you or whether they know anyone who does this kind of work and what that person's experiences have been. Conversations like this plant a seed: These people now think of you as a job seeker in that career field and may later relay to you news of a job opening. More likely, they will be able to tell you the name of someone who is more knowledgeable about the field you have in mind, and *that* person may be your actual lead for a job opening. Make a point of asking for the name of someone who knows lots of people in the field you're targeting. Studies of networks show that most contacts are made through a small number of very well-connected people.

Networking will probably be easier if your sequel career goal is in the industry where you already have experience and connections—for example, if you're moving into sales or communications within that field. Over the years, you have built up a network of contacts in that industry. You may actually know people who work in the precise job function that interests you. If not, you probably know people who know them.

Even if you're contemplating a sequel career in a different field, your industry connections can be useful. Other people are likely to have made a similar career move, so you may get in touch with them. Also, to the extent that the career is a sequel, the workers maintain contact with your familiar industry. For example, trainers are working in the education industry to prepare people for work in your familiar industry, and technical writers are publishing how-to books that teach industry-related skills. Someone in your industry has a relationship with those sequel-career workers.

No matter what industry interests you, a good place to start is LinkedIn. com, a website designed for networking. If you have not already joined, you may find it a useful way of connecting with friends, former classmates, and former business associates to let them know your career interests. The site offers tools for getting your contacts to write recommendations for you and for helping you get in touch with their contacts. You'll be especially interested in joining a LinkedIn group related to your industry. (If one doesn't exist, you can start one.) On the group page, you can participate in discussion of industry issues, read news about industry events and organizations, and find postings of job openings.

Be sure not to limit your networking to the Web. Face-to-face networking can be very powerful, so try to find local chapters of industry-related groups. Some local organizations that don't have a national profile may be active in your community; search for them at www.meetup.com. Many of these organizations are looking for volunteers or holding regular meetings. You also can do face-to-face networking on lunch dates.

If you can't find an appropriate group meeting, are too busy to take lunch breaks, and dislike Web-based networking, at least pick up the telephone and build your network that way.

Still one more way to build your network is to start a small business that disseminates information about your industry in blogs, podcasts, a business directory, or some other channel. As Chapter 6 explains, being a center of industry information will expand both your awareness of opportunities and your industry's awareness of you.

Cold-Calling Employers

Someone in your network may mention your name to a manager who is hiring for a job, and that person may give you a call. But, in many situations, the person in your network will give you the name of someone who is hiring, and it will be up to you to make the call. In that case, you are shifting to the cold-calling strategy.

You don't have to wait for your network to turn up likely employers to call. The most effective way to conduct a cold-calling campaign is to research the businesses that hire people for the kind of job you seek. If you are looking for work within your familiar industry, you probably already know many of these businesses. If not, professional associations also can be very helpful. Scan the association's membership directory and note which companies employ a lot of members. Another clue is to observe which businesses sponsor the association or its activities. But don't overlook small employers. You can find them listed in business directories such as the Yellow Pages.

When you have identified a likely business, don't contact the human resources department; they know only about the part of the job market that isn't hidden. Instead, find the name and phone number of someone who has the power to make a hiring decision. In a small company, this may be the CEO or other top manager; in a large company, it may be a department head. Telephone this person. If you call between 8 and 9 in the morning or 5 and 6 in the evening, you may improve the odds that the phone will be answered by the person you seek rather than by a secretary. If you get the person's voice mailbox, hang up and try again at another time; cold calls are unlikely to be returned. E-mail takes less courage than the telephone, but it is too easily lost in the pile of messages cluttering your target's inbox and may automatically be flagged as spam.

When you are talking to a person who can make a hiring decision, you have two tactics open to you: direct and indirect. The direct method is to give your elevator speech, make it clear that you are interested in a job, and ask for an interview. Be prepared to ask several times, because this shows your interest and determination. Don't ask whether the business has job openings, but perhaps ask if the business is likely to have openings in the future. If the person on the other end says that the company is not hiring now, ask for a get-acquainted interview—maybe a lunch date. At the very least, ask for leads to people who might be hiring for relevant jobs elsewhere, call those leads, and tell them who referred you. Expect a lot of rejection, but keep in mind that these calls take only a few minutes, so you can cover a large number of employers in one afternoon.

The indirect method is similar—it uses an elevator speech about your background and aims for an interview—but it stops short of asking for a *job* interview. Instead, you treat the person like a highly targeted networking contact; the goal is an interview that will focus on *learning more information* rather than on being hired. For example, you might say that you are thinking of specializing in the kind of work that goes on in that person's business and you want to learn more about the pros and cons of that specialization. If the person on the other end tries to cut you off by saying that the company is not hiring, make it clear that you are not asking for a job interview–you want information or perhaps advice. The informational interview may not, in fact, lead to a job at that company—at least not at present—but it may lead to a future job offer, and at least it has a good chance of taking your networking campaign to a higher level. This person is much more likely than your second cousin or your high school friend to know someone in another department or a similar business who has a job opening.

Job Postings

Although most job openings are not posted, and advertised jobs attract a lot of competing job candidates, you may want to spend some of your job-hunting time looking at postings. Don't limit yourself to general-purpose or industry-specific job boards; also look at the websites of employers. Often the home page will feature a link called "Careers" that leads to postings of current job openings, some of which may not be listed elsewhere.

Note that these job postings can also be useful leads for cold calls. The jobs that an employer advertises may be too high-level for you (Executive Director), too low-level for you (unpaid intern), or just not in your area of specialization, but the same employer may be hiring for additional jobs that are not posted (or not posted *yet*). Or the employer may know of a job available elsewhere. So use job postings as leads for cold calls.

Job Hunting Is a Job

Accept the idea that job hunting is a job in itself. Make a schedule of your job-hunting activities and stick to it. It helps to schedule differing activities in the same day, partly because some activities work best at specific times of day and partly because you can get bored and discouraged if you spend the whole day doing only one kind of job-hunting task.

Coping with Age Discrimination

Your accumulated experience can be the basis of a rewarding sequel career, but it can also lead to age discrimination when you try to land a job. Employers don't admit when they are practicing age discrimination because it's against the law, and they often hide behind justifications that sound legitimate. They may say the younger job candidate will demand a lower salary, will have more energy, will be easier to supervise. It doesn't matter whether or not these assertions are true or are legally justifiable reasons for a hiring decision; they exist, and you have little chance of being able to contest them in court.

Your best strategy for counteracting age discrimination is to project a younger image. This is partly a matter of appearance. Take a critical look at the clothes and hairstyle you wear and compare them to contemporary fashions. People who talk to you usually look into your eyes, so eyeglasses that are badly out of fashion can hurt your image. So can weight gain. You have to decide for yourself where to draw the line with highly personal (and perhaps costly) makeovers such as hair coloring, Botox, or plastic surgery; each person has a different comfort level.

Your appearance says a lot, but your skills and attitudes also need to be up to date. You need to be conversant with the latest technologies in your industry or any industry you're considering entering. It's especially important for you to be able to use the current technologies for communications. The last couple of decades have seen the shift from letters to fax and e-mail, next to instant messaging and cell phones, and now to texting and social networks. If you project the attitude that these channels of communication are faddish and that the old way still works just fine, you're diminishing your chances of getting hired. The same applies to the attitude you show regarding what kinds of people belong in your workplace. If your behavior or remarks show an outlook that's not inclusive of people from many backgrounds, you may exclude yourself from many opportunities.

Now Get Started on Your Sequel

It may take courage to leave your present job—or adjust to having lost it—and now use your accumulated knowledge in some new way. But the career change may lead to satisfactions that you've been missing until now.

It helps to keep thinking about your career in terms of the central metaphor of this book: **the sequel**. You may want to call your sequel "[insert your name here] Returns," "[insert your name here] Strikes Back," or "[insert your name here]: The Adventure Continues." Or maybe name it "[insert your name here]: Beyond [insert your previous job title here]."

It doesn't matter if your previous job had an ending that was unhappy or a letdown; the sequel can be much better. What you've been doing until now is not the whole story of your career. It's just one chapter in the narrative arc of your continuing adventures.

Where the Information Comes From

The information for this book comes from two major government sources:

- **The U.S. Department of Labor:** Much of the detailed information about occupations comes from the U.S. Department of Labor's O*NET database. The O*NET includes information on about 950 occupations and is now the primary source of detailed information on occupations. The Labor Department updates the O*NET on a regular basis, and this book uses the most recent one available, release 15. Information about earnings, growth, and number of openings is based on sources at the U.S. Department of Labor's Bureau of Labor Statistics (BLS). The Occupational Employment Statistics survey provided reliable figures on earnings, and the Employment Projections program provided the nation's best figures on job growth and openings. These two BLS programs use a slightly less detailed system of job titles than the O*NET does, but these titles can readily be linked to equivalent titles in the O*NET database.

- **The U.S. Census Bureau:** Data on the demographic characteristics of workers (percentage of women and average age) came from the Current Population Survey (CPS), conducted by the U.S. Census Bureau. As with the earnings and outlook data from the BLS, the CPS data was reported for a slightly different set of job titles, but it was usually possible to match these titles to the O*NET jobs.

Understand the Limits of the Data in This Book

As you look at the figures in this book, keep in mind that they are estimates. They give you a general idea about the number of workers employed, annual earnings, rate of job growth, and annual job openings.

Understand that a problem with such data is that it describes an average. Just as there is no precisely average person, there is no such thing as a statistically average example of a particular job. The data, while helpful, can also be misleading.

Take, for example, the yearly earnings information in this book. This is highly reliable data obtained from a very large U.S. working population sample by the Bureau of Labor Statistics. It tells you the average annual pay received as of May 2009 by people in various job titles. But this average is actually median annual pay, which means that half earned more and half less. Very few people earned exactly the median amount. Workers with little work experience and workers living in low-wage communities probably earned less. Workers who entered the occupation as a sequel probably had higher skills and commanded a higher wage.

Also keep in mind that the figures for job growth and number of openings are projections by labor economists—their best guesses about what the nation can expect between now and 2018. These projections are not guarantees. A catastrophic economic downturn, war, or technological breakthrough could change the actual outcome.

Finally, don't forget that the job market consists of both job openings and job *seekers*. The figures on job growth and openings don't tell you how many people will be competing with you to be hired. In some (but not all) job descriptions, the "Employment Outlook" statement gives you an indication of the level of competition. To be fully informed about this matter, you should speak to people who educate or train tomorrow's workers; they probably have a good idea of how many graduates and trainees find rewarding employment and how quickly. People in the workforce can provide insights into this issue as well. Use your critical thinking skills to evaluate what people tell you. For example, educators or trainers may be trying to recruit you, whereas people in the workforce may be trying to discourage you from competing. Get a variety of opinions to balance out possible biases.

So, in reviewing the information in this book, please understand the limitations of the data. You need to use common sense in career decision making as in most other things in life.

Data Complexities

Here are further details about where the figures come from and how they are computed.

Earnings

The employment security agency of each state gathers information on earnings for various jobs and forwards it to the U.S. Bureau of Labor Statistics. This information is organized in standardized ways by a BLS program called Occupational Employment Statistics, or OES. To keep the earnings for the various jobs and regions comparable, the OES screens out certain types of earnings and includes others, so the OES earnings used in this book represent straight-time gross pay exclusive of premium pay. More specifically, the OES earnings include each job's base rate; cost-of-living allowances; guaranteed pay; hazardous-duty pay; incentive pay, including commissions and production bonuses; on-call pay; and tips. The OES earnings do not include back pay, jury duty pay, overtime pay, severance pay, shift differentials, nonproduction bonuses, or tuition reimbursements. Also, self-employed workers are not included in the estimates, and they can be a significant segment in certain occupations.

In each job description, you'll find two topics related to earnings:

- The Annual Earnings figure shows the median earnings (half earn more, half earn less) for May 2009.

- The statement of Earnings Growth Potential is a verbal phrase representing the ratio between the 10th percentile and the median. In a job with "very high" potential (such as Real Estate Brokers), you have great opportunity for increasing your earnings as you gain experience and skills. When the potential of the job is "very low" (as it is for Legislators), you will probably need to move on to another occupation to improve your earnings substantially. Because the percentage figures would be hard to interpret, the book uses verbal tags to indicate the level of Earnings Growth Potential: "very low" when the percentage is less than 25%, "low" for 25%–35%, "medium" for 35%–40%, "high" for 40%–50%, and "very high" for any figure higher than 50%.

The median earnings for all workers in all occupations were $43,460 in May 2009. The 100 jobs with detailed descriptions in this book tend to require a high level of skill, so their average is higher: $59,764. (This is a weighted average, which means that jobs with larger workforces are given greater weight in the computation.)

The earnings data from the OES survey is reported under a system of job titles called the Standard Occupational Classification system, or SOC. Most of these jobs have an exact counterpart in the O*NET system of job titles that appear in the job descriptions. In some cases, however, an SOC title cross-references to more than one O*NET job title. For example, the O*NET has separate information for Copy Writers and for Poets, Lyricists, and Creative Writers, but the BLS reports earnings for a single SOC occupation called Writers and Authors. Therefore, you may notice that the salary figures that appear for these two specializations ($46,270) are identical. In reality, there probably are differences, but this is the most detailed information available.

Projected Growth and Number of Job Openings

This information comes from the Office of Occupational Statistics and Employment Projections, a program within the Bureau of Labor Statistics that develops information about projected trends in the nation's labor market for the next 10 years. The most recent projections, taken from a publication called *Occupational Projections and Training Data (OPTD)*, cover the years from 2008 to 2018. The projections are based on information about people moving into and out of occupations. The BLS uses data from various sources in projecting the growth and number of openings for each job title—some data comes from the Census Bureau's Current Population Survey and some comes from an OES survey. The BLS economists assumed a steady economy with no major war, depression, or other upheaval. They also assumed that recessions may occur during the decade covered by these projections, as would be consistent with the business cycles the nation has experienced for several decades. However, because the projections cover 10 years, the figures for job growth and openings are intended to provide an average of both the good times and the bad times.

Like the earnings figures, the figures on projected growth and job openings are reported according to the SOC classification. So, again, you'll sometimes find O*NET occupational titles that share the same outlook figures. To continue the example given earlier, you'll notice that Copy Writers have projected growth of 14.8% and 5,420 projected job openings, the same figures given for Poets, Lyricists, and Creative Writers. You should realize that the 14.8% rate of projected growth represents the *average* of these two occupations—one may actually experience higher growth than the other—and that these two occupations will *share* the 5,420 projected openings. (A note appears to indicate when such sharing exists.)

For the 12 postsecondary teaching occupations (all of which are described in Chapter 3), the figures for job growth and annual job openings are based on some special calculations. The only figures available from the Department of Labor apply to a combination of 38 postsecondary teaching jobs. The trends of the last several years show that none of these jobs grew or took on workers at a significantly faster rate than the other 37. Neither is there reason to think that any of them has much higher or lower job turnover than any other. Therefore, the assumption for these jobs is that they all will share the same rate of projected job growth, 15.1%, and that the number of job openings for each occupation will be proportional to the size of the workforce. To compute each occupation's share of the 55,290 projected job openings for the 38 jobs, I used the ratio of the workforce size of each occupation to the workforce size of the combined occupation (1,699,180).

Job-growth figures may not be as easy to interpret as salary figures. For example, is projected growth of 12% good or bad? Keep in mind that the average (mean) growth projected for all occupations by the Bureau of Labor Statistics is 10.1%. One-quarter of the SOC occupations have a growth projection of 1.0% or lower. Growth of 9.6% is the median, meaning that half of the occupations have more, half less. Only one-quarter of the occupations have growth projected at more than 15.1%.

It's not as important to get an impression of what an average number of projected job openings might be. Keep in mind that the occupations in our economy with the largest numbers of job openings have low skill requirements and offer many openings simply because the turnover of workers is very fast. (Think, for example, of the restless young burger-flippers at your local McDonald's.) Compare projected openings for one occupation you're considering with openings for another job you're considering, not with some average.

Perhaps you're wondering why the descriptions include figures for both job growth *and* number of openings. Aren't these two ways of saying the same thing? Actually, you need to know both. Consider the occupation Agents and Business Managers of Artists, Performers, and Athletes, which is projected to grow at the impressive rate of 22.4%. There should be lots of opportunities in such a fast-growing job, right? Not exactly. This is a small occupation, with only about 11,700 people currently employed. So, even though it is growing rapidly, it will not create many new jobs (about 1,000 per year). Now consider First-Line Supervisors/Managers of Retail Sales Workers. This occupation is growing at the lukewarm rate of 5.2%. Nevertheless, this is a huge occupation that employs more than 1.63 million workers. So, even though its growth rate is unimpressive, it is expected to take on more than 45,000 new workers each year as existing workers retire, die, or move on to other jobs. That's why you'll find both of these economic indicators for each occupation and why you should pay attention to both.

Information About the Sequels

Chapters 2 through 8 describe some prominent types of sequel careers. In each chapter, you'll find lists of the important work activities and the factors that characterize the work environment. These information topics are both based on O*NET data. The ratings in the O*NET database are weighted, which means that jobs with larger workforce size are given greater weight in the calculations.

A table at the end of Chapter 1 shows prominent skills that characterize the sequels described in these chapters. The skill profiles of the seven sequels are somewhat similar, so this table is based on the *difference* between each sequel's profile and the average profile for all the sequel careers. This methodology emphasizes the skills that differentiate each sequel from the others.

Information in the Job Descriptions

The job descriptions are based on the most current information from a variety of government sources.

- **Job Title:** This is the job title for the job as defined by the U.S. Department of Labor and used in its O*NET database.

- **Data Elements:** The information on earnings, earnings growth potential, growth, and annual openings comes from various government databases, as explained earlier in this appendix. The figures for percentage of self-employed workers are derived from the *Occupational Projections and Training Data (OPTD)* report.

- **Summary Description and Tasks:** The first part of each job description provides a summary of the occupation in bold type. It is followed by a listing of tasks that are generally performed by people who work in the job. This information comes from the O*NET database; where necessary, tasks are edited to keep them from exceeding 1,000 characters.

- **Skills:** The O*NET database provides data on 35 skills, but that level of detail would not be helpful. Instead, the job description identifies any skill with a rating for level of mastery that is higher than the average rating for this skill for all jobs and a rating for importance that is higher than very low. Skills are ordered by the amount by which their ratings exceed the average rating for all occupations, from highest to lowest. If there are more than 8 such skills, you'll find only those 8 with the highest ratings. The skills are defined later in this appendix.

- **Personality Type:** Job descriptions include the name of the related personality types, based on O*NET information. These personality types were originally developed by John Holland and are used in the *Self-Directed Search (SDS)* and other career assessment inventories and information systems.

- **Education of Workforce:** These figures are derived from the *OPTD* report. Note that they describe all people presently in the workforce, not just new hires. In some cases, new hires fresh out of school may be expected to hold higher-level degrees than many long-time employees possess. On the other hand, educational requirements may be lower for those entering with a lot of work experience.

- **Average Age:** This information is based on data from the Current Population Survey. The average presented here is a numerical mean. In some cases, the Census Bureau does not report the information at the same level of detail as the O*NET, and the figure represents the average for a small group of occupations (for example, the CPS reports on Loan Counselors and Officers as a single title rather than as two separate occupations).

- **Percentage of Women:** This information is based on the same source as the average age and also sometimes represents the average for a small group of occupations. The Census does not report any figure for occupations with small workforces, so no data was available for several occupations in this book.

- **Work Environment:** This information is based on "work context" ratings in the O*NET database. Work conditions that appear here have a rating that exceeded the midpoint of the rating scale. The order does not indicate any condition's frequency on the job. Consider whether you like these conditions and whether any of these conditions would make you uncomfortable. Keep in mind that when hazards are present (for example, contaminants), protective equipment and procedures are provided to keep you safe.

Getting all the information we used in the job descriptions was not a simple process, and it is not always perfect. Even so, the descriptions are based on the best and most recent sources of data available.

Definitions of Skills

These skills, from the O*NET database, are used in the job descriptions. They also appear in the table at the end of Chapter 1.

Basic Skills	These skills facilitate learning or the more rapid acquisition of knowledge.
Active Learning	Working with new material or information to grasp its implications.
Active Listening	Listening to what other people are saying and asking questions as appropriate.
Critical Thinking	Using logic and analysis to identify the strengths and weaknesses of different approaches.
Learning Strategies	Using multiple approaches when learning or teaching new things.
Mathematics	Using mathematics to solve problems.
Monitoring	Assessing how well one is doing when learning or doing something.
Reading Comprehension	Understanding written sentences and paragraphs in work-related documents.
Science	Using scientific methods to solve problems.
Speaking	Talking to others to effectively convey information.
Writing	Communicating effectively with others in writing as indicated by the needs of the audience.

Cross-Functional Skills	These skills facilitate performance in a variety of job settings.
Complex Problem Solving	Identifying complex problems, reviewing the options, and implementing solutions.
Coordination	Adjusting actions in relation to others' actions.
Equipment Maintenance	Performing routine maintenance and determining when and what kind of maintenance is needed.
Equipment Selection	Determining the kinds of tools and equipment needed to do a job.
Installation	Installing equipment, machines, wiring, or programs to meet specifications.
Instructing	Teaching others how to do something.
Judgment and Decision Making	Weighing the relative costs and benefits of a potential action.
Management of Financial Resources	Determining how money will be spent to get the work done and accounting for these expenditures.
Management of Material Resources	Obtaining and seeing to the appropriate use of equipment, facilities, and materials needed to do certain work.
Management of Personnel Resources	Motivating, developing, and directing people as they work; identifying the best people for the job.
Negotiation	Bringing others together and trying to reconcile differences.
Operation and Control	Controlling operations of equipment or systems.
Operation Monitoring	Watching gauges, dials, or other indicators to make sure a machine is working properly.
Operations Analysis	Analyzing needs and product requirements to create a design.
Persuasion	Persuading others to approach things differently.

Programming	Writing computer programs for various purposes.
Quality Control Analysis	Evaluating the quality or performance of products, services, or processes.
Repairing	Repairing machines or systems, using the needed tools.
Service Orientation	Actively looking for ways to help people.
Social Perceptiveness	Being aware of others' reactions and understanding why they react the way they do.
Systems Analysis	Determining how a system should work and how changes will affect outcomes.
Systems Evaluation	Looking at many indicators of system performance and taking into account their accuracy.
Technology Design	Generating or adapting equipment and technology to serve user needs.
Time Management	Managing one's own time and the time of others.
Troubleshooting	Determining what is causing an operating error and deciding what to do about it.

Index

M

The Sequel: How to Change Your Career Without Starting Over

T

© JIST Works   The Sequel: How to Change Your Career Without Starting Over

U–V

W–Z